We Are The Kitties

...And We Writed You This Book

INKBLOT BOOKS

We Are The Kitties
...And We Writed You This Book

All Rights Reserved © 2007 Inkblot Books

No part of this book may be reproduced or transmitted in any form or by any means, without permission in writing from the publisher.

Published by Inkblot Books
www.inkblotbooks.com
ISBN 1-932461-14-0

Cover image © 2007 Jane Schumacher

Published in the United States of America

We Are The Kitties
...And We Writed You This Book

Beau Davis

Thank You for buying it.
We hope you enjoy it.

The Kitties Of The Blogosphere

Dedicated to the memory of our friends who have gone to wait for us at the Rainbow Bridge.

Norton, Trixie, Bear, Gizzy, Chatham, Buzzerbee, Anastasia, Oscar the Puppy Cat, Ubee, Brendan, Eddie, Eponine, Digby, Ullrick, Butterscotch, Jasmine, Whisper, Miss Piggy, Georgia, Jupiter, Whisper, Mia, Purrsident Larry ... and so many others that our broken hearts can't count.

We miss you.

Table Of Contents

1-Detective Skeeter Cold Case #27 by Skeeter
8-Haikus by Beau
10-Angels Of The Rainbow Bridge by C.D. Smith
42-Catwalk by Laurie Jones
43-Craptacular…In The Literal Sense by Fi-Fi
47-Me And My Alter Ego by Hendrix The Kitty
51-Home by brandi
52-Oh, The Horror! By Bonnie Underfoot
55-brandi by Carol Z
56-What I've Learned About Life by Puff
60-In Silence… by Brenda Bentley
61-My First Five Days by HRH Yao-Lin
64-Windy Day by Karen Jo Gray
65-What I Learned About The Early History Of Northamerica by Ko Ko Schumacher
69-Wendell's Food Haikus by Wendell Entin
71-Discover by Dee Francis
75-1,018 Is My Lucky Number by Perfectly Parker
84-Reeport Of Findings On Reeserch Into Gravity Free Zones by Dr. Buddy Longwhiskers
90-LC, Mighty Hunter by LC
92-Me And My Kitty Cats by Dee Francis
93-Skeeter Says: by Skeeter
95-Of Memory And Loss by C.D. Smith
97-Winter by Jessica Forward

98-Aliens by Sammy Meezer
100-Haiku For You by Colette Werner
103-Interludes by The Missouri Meowers
107-How To Train Your Human Slave by HRH Yao-Lin
112-Mom by Merlin Schumacher
117-The Ideal Gift For Your Human by HRH Yao-Lin
119-An Introduction To Baby Mao by Baby Mao
120-Casper by Dean McCaughan
121-Sometimes by Tilli
123-An Introduction to The Siamese Cat by HRH Yao-Lin
125-Songs Of Torment Of Stinky Brothers by Shadow Schumacher
128-My Life With Kitty-Cats by E.J. Smith
139-Ode To Cod by Edsel The Pooch
140-You Know You're A Cat Blogger When… by Baby Mao's Mummy
143-Calendar Cats by Karen Jo Gray
146-Aliens Amongst Us by Dee Francis
148-A Meezer's Thoughts by Miles Meezer
149-A Tribute To Mao's Testicles by Baby Mao
150-Mooch—Feline Hobo, Beloved Friend by Shawna Howes
166-It's A Four Letter Word… by Max the Psychokitty
177-How Can I Be Losted? By Buddah Pest
183-The 31 by Max the Psychokitty
189-Kitties Of The Blogoshere – A Pictorial

Detective Skeeter
Cold Case #27
Skeeter

I was zonked out on the sunny windowsill of my run down flea-bitten office when someone came banging on the office door. It always starts that way. Between the first bang and the second I was sittin at my desk poring over some fake documents I kept around for the purpose, lookin professional. After enough years in the detective biz, ya learn some tricks, ya know?

So by the time the visitor got through the door, I looked like I had been pretty bizy with serious work. Oh mouse-droppings, it was Lt Woof again. Now, I got nothin against Lt Woof. He's a good police dog and a steady type. Trustworthy, loyal, yadda, yadda, yadda. But he's a messenger. I knew who hadda be down in the car waitin (an too embarrassed to show himself)... Old fat Capn Katz, stuck onna cold case, getting pressure from some top Bein, and desperate for help.

Well, that's why they come here. I'm the cat of last resort, the last one they go to when they run out of ideas. I'm the burier of cold cases, the last one you go to when you got nowhere else to go, the "final solution" for the crimes ya can't solve on yer own (oh hairballs, I'm readin my business card out loud again. I really gotta stop doing that).

But seriously, I'm the cat ya go to when all else fails. I've made a career outta it. I get paid top dollop to notice what no one else does. I solve cold crimes. If I didn't blow it all on primo nip, heavy cream, fast kitties, and slow dogs at the track, I'd be a millionaire. I bet I'm on my 8th life by now.

So the big sniffie was here with a job... Good. I was outta the primo nip an down to the Wal-Mart stuff. I needed to rif a heavy gig. So the woofie barges in knockin half my furniture over on the way.

"OK, OK, Lt Woof" I says, "jus calm down and tell me the deal and stop beatin my plants to death wit yer tail"! He calmed down and pushed a folder over the desk. I opened it an started readin. I punctuated the silence with a few "Hmms" an "I see"'s and some thoughtful paper-shufflin. I wasn't actually getting much from the folder info, but I know from past experience it impresses Lt Woofie no end.

"OK Woof, I'll take the case. But tell Katz down in the car that he's gotta give me transport and an open-ended expense account." Woof's ears fell flat to his head on that. He said Katz wouldn't go for that an he didn't dare even bring him that demand. Well actually, it was "Whine whine sniff whine howl" but ya gotta translate sometimes. I speak 3 kinna cat, 2 woofies, and I can get by with some birds. Even a little squirrel if I lip-read some. So I told Woof the demand would be eagerly accepted

And We Writed You This Book 3

and he wouldn't be told "bad dog" or anything like that.

Sure enough, he came back the next day all happy an excited. More importantly, with first class train tickets (one way, I noted sourly) and a Letter of Credit from Capn Katz (Oh good, primo nip again). I was surprised at the destination, though. The folder from Woof had said "missing kid" and I assumed it was a goat. This was a Bein address an I wasn't expectin that. Well, maybe they had a missing goat, but I wasn't gonna bet a mouse on THAT!

The trip to the Famous Old Place was nice, 1st class all the way. I sipped some subtle nip tea and watched a rare Tom and Jerry movie (Tom won)! There was a carriage (A CARRIAGE!) waitin for me at the station. As I was conveyed (ooh) up the long private driveway, I wondered if I was in over my head. Beins can be very tricky an confoozin!

Old Mr. Famous was there to greet me at the door (after I was passed along by 3 butlers). "At the door" means about 100 pounces away, but I understood it meant he was VERY personally concerned. As we sat in the Study, he filled in the gaps fom Woof's folder. There were details I could not know until I was fully involved in the case. I was quite surprised. Few crimes are so "hiss-hiss" that I never even hear of them.

Apparently, Mr. Famous's grandson had vanished some 100 Big Moons ago. It was assumed to be a squirreled ransom case, but Old Famous had begun to suspect it was a family job. When I expressed some mild surprise at this, he merely whispered "inheritance". I nodded wisely and made a note to ask Capn Katz what "inheritance" was. It sounded serious though. Hey, if "inheritance" was important to Mr. Famous, it was serious to me. Motives come from strange places; sometimes even Old Famous ones…

Old Man Famous proceeded to divulge some family secrets and I cant mention those so as to protect the non-criminally innocent Beins. I can assure you that none of them was truly "innocent" but almost all of them were "legal", if ya get what I mean. After that, I had the run of the property and nearly anythin Old Man Famous owned (Oh cool GOLF CARTS)!

So I wandered aroun the Famous Old Place for a while (I actually thought of calling for Lt Woof; he does have a great nose). But he is sometimes, shall we say, too obvious in his goals, so I decided to seek a more logical conclusion.

After a week of traipsing around the Old Famous Place talking (purring at) the family, spying on the paid slaves (sorry; butlers, maids, etc), looking for clues, sniffing around as best I could I was pretty much baffled. It was embarrassing (the wealth and exorbitant riches, I mean – and none of them were mine).

It sure wasn't a total loss. I ate tuna nearly every day (with ham an shimp sides on most occassions). I drank heavy cream when I wanted. When Old Famous Man asked about "progress" I tried to go vague and positive, ya know?

I did see lots of interesting things aroun the

place. The survivin grandkid had a pot patch in a far corner of the property (coupla thousand backyards wide an long). It was a long walk an he dint dare use Daddy's golf carts (an he thought a golf cart would drive through the woods anyway, ROTFLMAO). The kid was too much a clueless sap to have committed a crime. But apparent cluelessness can hide cleverness…

One of the maids had a secret little shack where she earned extra money somehow (I never did quite figure that one out). Maybe the men who visited helped her spin flax into gold or somethin. It would have been simpler to follow the cook who had found a stream with shiny gold things that Beins like a lot.

Old Lady Famous had a place where she gardened. As gardens go, is was pretty poor. There was a nice tiny water path through the center that was nice to drink from. But there were tiny dead sticks at the house end. And tiny little everygreen seedlings on the other side of the stream. A little empty place. Some tiny litle flowers toward the bottom an a little tiny rock where the stream went inna the "lake." Pretty little girly stuff fer an old Famous Lady, I thought. It wasn't a very nice-lookin garden (not that I garden myself, but I have seen pictures of nice gardens).

The coachman had his own little secret (he thought). A circle inna woods where people came an danced wifout their clothes… LOL! He thought it was all weird an spooky, but I thought it was jus normal. What's the deal on cloths anyway?

Well, they all had problems and none of them led me to any clues. I had to admit defeat. After a half a Big Moon enjoyin Old Man Famous's nip tea and tuna, I told him; I hadn't solved the case. He was disappointed. But I felt bitter about it. I had never failed before. Of course, I hadn't had to solve Bein problems before. I'm good at findin the missin kitty or figurin out who stole the cheese, which woofie bit which other one first even a few years ago, etc. But, no not this time. I called Capn Katz for a helicopter out and back home, reputation in ruins.

The helicopter arrived an on I went. The Famous mansion grew smaller as we ascended, the secrets of the (mostly) innocent ones came in sight. I watched as the nice stream flowed into the lake an I could see odd dead trees at the north. It was a sad ignominous departure. The maid's little cabin faded from view in the evergreen trees on the other side of the stream. Finally, there were just the magificent azaleas where the stream hit the lake near the boulder. "Dismal", I thought to myself.

Capn Katz had made sure to be along for the ride. He was so annoyingly triumphant. "Hey Skeeterkins" he yelled over the noise of the ear-crushing thump of the blades, "how'd ya do on THIS ONE Flatpaw?".

"Not bad" I screamed back, "I've solved it. Return us to the Old Famous Place". Oh kitties! Ya should seen the look on his face. Some of his fur actually fell off! You'd have thought Lt Woof suddenly thought he was bacon!

And We Writed You This Book

Back at the mansion, Old Famous brought out his freshest heavy cream and most potent nip. I was the center of attention, the equal of the Beins, and the superior of Capn Katz once again.. I was IT!

"The solution is simple, my dear Katz. Old Famous Lady had contructed a replica of her dear son's burial place in her own garden. I had detected several "wrong" smells in her garden and decieved Capn Katz into providing me with the last information required, an aerial view. Lady Famous learned that the entire estate was to go to Mr. Famous's son and she determined to get rid of him. But as he was her child also, she couldn't help but construct a memorial. Her garden was a duplicate of the property and the large stone was where the body was buried. She had him killed but, as her child, she could not not identify his final resting place."

"QED, heh, Katz"? I'll take the rest of the payment now, please an thank you.

(Hey readers, we won't tell anyone I didn't have a clue until I was leavin in the helicopter, OK? I gotta reputation to protekt…)

I used up all the money from the Old Famous case on "stuff", OK? I was zonked out on the sunny windowsill of my run down flea-bitten office when someone came banging on the office door. It always starts that way. Between the first bang and the second I was sittin at my desk poring over some fake documents I kept around for the purpose, lookin professional. After enough years in the detective biz, ya learn some tricks, ya know?

Detective Skeeter

HAIKUS
by Beau

<u>NAPPING</u>
Sun spots, cozy laps
My favorite places to nap
Napping is the best!

<u>MOM</u>
I really love mom.
She takes real good care of me!
Mom is my best friend!

<u>PLAYTIME</u>
Mice and catnip toys,
Feather and squishy balls, too!
Oh, so much to do!

BLOGGING
I've so much to say.
A blogging cat I will be!
MOOOM! A laptop pleeeease!!

CRAZIES
Running down the hall
Leaping, jumping, and flipping!
Oh crazies feel so good!

LOOK! Out There
Chitter Chitter Chit!
Oh boy oh boy!   It's a bird!
I love to bird watch!

Angels of the Rainbow Bridge
C.D. Smith

A Bridge Constructed

Dulcinea watched as her angelic brother, Antonius, carried a silently sleeping kabble of kittens in his robe away from the center of heaven. She watched as he took them from the birthing grounds of all the kitten souls that God had created to the dark horizon that separated Heaven from Earth. She shook her head at Antonius' self appointed task. It will bring him nothing but sorrow and pain, Dulcinea thought. Dulcinea sighed.

It had been many eons since the Great Cast Out. Things had changed on Earth. Humans now ranged across its fertile breadth, and it was off limits to any Angel that did not have a True Purpose on its firmament. Antonius was one of those Angels who had found a True Purpose; he had chosen to take all of the kittens that were to be born from Heaven to their Earthly mothers. Dulcinea felt a most unangelic emotion, jealously, at Antonius' apparent joy at taking each kitten to Earth. Dulcinea had not yet found a True Purpose to allow her to travel between Heaven and Earth.

She was shaken from her self pity as a group of stern and fierce looking angels moved past her and half-flew, half-ran to the dark horizon. These were Guardian Angels. Another True Purpose that Dulcinea did not feel calling to her.

Dulcinea flew to the nearest edge of the dark horizon that separated Heaven from Earth. This was as far as she could go towards Earth without her own True Purpose. She watched many chosen Angels cross the boundary. She even saw Antonius cross more times than any other. He is going to wear himself out, Dulcinea thought.

As she pondered what true Purpose would let her cross the boundary between Heaven and Earth, Dulcinea thought she heard a small cry coming from the threshold of the boundary. She turned her ears towards the faint sound. It was low and soft; almost pleading in its nature. Dulcinea knew she had to find the source of that sound.

The boundary between Heaven and Earth flickered slightly and lightened to a hazy blue to her angelic eyes. There in the smoky haze was an older Ginger Tom who was favouring his right foreleg. He tried to move towards Dulcinea but something was preventing his passage. Dulcinea reached down and laid her hand upon the cat's head. She was rewarded with a deep throbbing purr and enthusiastic stretch towards her palm. Dulcinea noticed Antonius returning from Earth.

"Antonius." Dulcinea called to her brother. "There is one of your charges here."

Antonius flew to his sister's side and regarded the old Ginger Tom.

"I remember you." Antonius smiled. "You were given to the little Calico who lived in the Inn."

"How did he get here?" Dulcinea asked.

"I do not know." Antonius replied. "Maybe he followed me when I brought back some of his unwanted brothers and sisters."

"You only bring back the unwanted ones?" Dulcinea asked incredulously. "I thought you took all the kittens to Earth and brought back all the lost souls."

Antonius shook his head. "I do take all the kittens to Earth, but I only bring back those who have been forsaken by Mankind."

"What about those who have not been forsaken by humans?" Dulcinea asked.

"They wait to enter Heaven with those who loved them." Antonius responded.

"Where?" Dulcinea asked as she motioned towards the Dark Horizon. "Where do these creatures wait? In this hopeless darkness?"

"I am sorry, Dearest Dulcinea." Antonius responded. "That is not given to me to know. I wish I could help you fathom this riddle, but I have much to do."

Dulcinea looked at the smoky blue haze, the dark horizon and the Ginger Tom that seemed content to lie at her feet and play with the hem of her robe. This was not acceptable, she thought. This

Ginger Tom found me by accident; how many others are roaming the boundary and waiting for their humans to join them in Heaven.

Dulcinea reached down and scratched the Ginger Tom beneath his chin. "How long have you walked this Darkening Road, beloved friend?"

The Ginger Tom simply rolled onto his back and continued to play with her hem. Dulcinea's wings straightened and fluffed as her True Purpose dawned on her. She bent down and petted the Ginger Tom once more. Dulcinea assured him that she would be back. She flew to the center of Heaven with a request burning within her angelic heart.

Dulcinea sat at the edge of the boundary and played with the Ginger Tom. She had been given her True Purpose, but she did not know how to do it or what was required to fulfill it. Several other animals had shown up as she sat and played with the Ginger Tom; a rabbit, a horse, a bird and several rambunctious dogs. It was obvious that there were far more creatures caught in the boundary between Heaven and Earth.

There was a sudden brightening in the dark horizon and a single human appeared at the threshold of Heaven and Earth. Ginger Tom's ears perked up and the pain in his foreleg disappeared as he raced towards the human. The human picked up Ginger Tom and nuzzled him lovingly. Dulcinea felt another pang of jealousy, for as much as Ginger Tom purred and cuddled with her, this was the being that he waited for to take him away from the Boundary and into Heaven. A voice behind Dulcinea startled her.

"I thought he would keep him." Antonius mused. "I saw the potential within him the moment the kittens were born. I'm surprised he didn't keep them all."

"Antonius." Dulcinea turned. "How long have you been there?"

"Long enough to watch you play with every creature that dares to leave the darkness of the Boundary." Antonius held out his hand. "Come with me."

Antonius took Dulcinea across the Boundary to Earth. He knew what she asked of God and what his response was and he could see that she now had a True Purpose. He took her to one of his favourite spots on Earth, a vast meadow filled with flowers and grass.

"This is Earth?" Dulcinea asked.

"This is but one part of Earth." Antonius responded. "It is one of my favourites."

"Why did you bring me here?"

"You asked God to let you help those creatures waiting for their humans." Antonius replied. "I wanted to show you a small part of Earth to maybe help you with your True Purpose."

"Yes." Dulcinea thought out loud. "This is what the creatures waiting at the Boundary of Heaven need."

Dulcinea reached down and tried to grab a handful of the dirt and flowering plants. The soil and plants passed through her angelic fingers. Dulcinea tried again to picked up some of this earthly matter.

"You cannot touch it, Dulcinea." Antonius stated sensing his sister's frustration. "You and I are

And We Writed You This Book 15

not of this plane."

"But this is what I need to bring back." Dulcinea pleaded excitedly. "This is what all those creatures need to feel at ease and at peace until their humans come to Heaven."

"I do not know how to help you." Antonius replied. "It is up to you to find a way to bridge this Earthly world with ours."

Dulcinea walked the edge of the Boundary between Heaven and Earth. She could now see the countless animals that were waiting for their human friends to cross over into Heaven. Her heart trembled at the faint cries and lonely wails she heard.

Antonius was right. She had to find a way to bridge the Boundary between Heaven and Earth for these lost animal souls. The meadow he had shown her was exactly what she wanted for those lost souls; a place for them to rest and to play and wait for their beloved Humans to join them in Heaven. She had tried to create the meadow on this side of the Boundary, but the flowers and the grass faded away as soon as she turned her attention away from them. In Heaven, Dulcinea could create whatever she wished but it would only last as long as she concentrated on it. As soon as she thought of something else, her previous constructions would disappear.

Dulcinea went back to the meadow that Antonius had shown her. She sat amongst the flowers and the grasses and the plants. She breathed the earthly perfume of the mint plants and the summer flowers. This was want she needed to recreate. But this was God's creation, as an Angel she would never be able to match this. At best it would be a poor mockery of the original. Dulcinea was crestfallen. One of her feathers dropped from her wing as her melancholy took its toll on her spirit. It slowly drifted to the ground and came to rest on a small patch of grass.

Dulcinea watched as a windblown seed from a dandelion landed on her fallen feather. She tried to pick up the dandelion seed but it passed through her hand once again. Frustrated, Dulcinea picked up her feather that had fallen to the ground. She suddenly drew in a surprised breath. There on her discarded feather lay the dandelion seed.

"I cannot touch you." Dulcinea realized. "But my feathers, once fallen can."

Dulcinea reached towards her right wing and pulled another feather out. She used this second feather as a tiny broom and she swept some dirt onto her first feather's shimmering white surface. The dirt did not pass through. Dulcinea's heart beamed as she discovered how to bring the essence of the meadow back to the Boundary.

Dulcinea swept as much dirt onto the feather as it seemed to be able to hold. She flew back to Heaven as quickly as she dared, for fear of the dirt blowing off her discarded feather.

Dulcinea stood at the hazy edge of the Boundary and looked hopefully at the dirt that lay on top of her wing feather. She closed her eyes and gave praise to God as she deposited the dirt on the feather onto the firmament of Heaven at her feet. The firmament swirled like smoke as the dirt from Earth struck it.

Dulcinea looked down where the dirt had landed. It passed right through the swirling haze.

"It is gone." Dulcinea observed, as her heart sank.

Dulcinea flew back to the meadow with her two feathers clutched tightly in her hands. She swept more dirt from the Meadow onto their surface and carried them back to Heaven. She looked at the two feathers with the faint traces of Earth on them. Simply dropping the Earthly matter onto the Heavenly firmament did not work, Dulcinea thought.

She reached down and laid the two feathers side by side onto the Firmament. This time the dirt did not disappear through the heavenly ground. Instead the dirt deepened and thickened and a small patch of flowers and grass sprang up. Dulcinea did not have to recreate what God had created on Earth; she simply had to give it some angelic support.

Dulcinea flew back to the meadow. She reached back and pulled two feathers from her wings and swept more Earthly matter onto them. She took them back to Heaven and laid them next to the other two feathers. Once again the dirt deepened and thickened and more flowers and grass sprang up on the tiny space. Dulcinea rejoiced at the sight of the small patch of flowers and grass. Already, several creatures at the Boundary had begun to show up; drawn by the scent of the Earth they had left behind.

Dulcinea began making trips from Heaven to Earth and back again. Each time carrying two of her feathers covered in Earthy matter from the meadow. She soon had a small plot that was covered with plants and flowers and grass. It was also covered with animals that were waiting for their human masters.

Dulcinea looked at the small plot of ground she had made and the numbers of animals that mulled at the edge trying to find a spot where they could rest. She looked at her wings. She had not realized but both were thin and bloody. In her zeal to create this spot, she had pulled feathers faster than she was able to replace them. If she kept this pace, she would not have any feathers left in her wings, and once that happened, she would no longer be able to move about Heaven as an Angel. Dulcinea dropped her chin to her chest and softly cried at her failure.

Antonius saw his sister as she stood sobbing at the edge of her tiny meadow. He hesitated but a moment as the recently winged kittens within his robed struggled to be free. Antonius smiled and took his charges to their new heavenly home. Once his work was done he returned to his sister's side.

"Dulcinea." Antonius said sharply. "Why have you stopped? I see that you have found a way to bring the Earthly meadow to Heaven, but it is far too small for all the creatures that need it."

"I cannot do any more, Antonius." Dulcinea motioned towards her tattered wings. "To do even this much is more than I can handle. I will have to wait until my feathers grow back. Then I will start again."

"Then what will you do with all this?" Antonius motioned towards the immense pile of angelic feathers.

Dulcinea looked up a saw an immense pile

of angelic wing feathers. She had been so lost in her grief at failing at her True Purpose she had not seen the pile grow.

"How?" Dulcinea asked.

Before Antonius could answer, Dulcinea watched as four Guardian Angels flew past. As they passed the great pile of feathers, they each tore a handful of their own feathers from their wings and cast them onto the pile. Dulcinea smiled as she saw a group of Cherubim also pull several of their tiny feathers and add them to the pile.

"I told the Angelic Host of your True Purpose," Antonius said. "And of your lack of wing feathers. Your brothers and sisters have chosen to help you fulfill your True Purpose."

Antonius reached towards his wings and was about to add his own feathers to the pile. Dulcinea reached over and stopped him.

"Your feathers have another purpose." Dulcinea stated with a smile. "As you have provided a heavenly path to the Unwanted and Lost Ones, I will provide the path for Those Who Wait."

Dulcinea took each and every feather in the great pile and used them to produce an earthly Meadow that stretched as far as the human eye could see across Heaven. It was a piece of Earth supported on the wings of Angels. Dulcinea looked at the meadow and the countless creatures that now moved freely in the flowers and grass. Some limped, some moved very slowly. Dulcinea knew her True Purpose had one more price.

Dulcinea took the last two feathers that she

had brought from Earth and held them in front of her. Two tears fell from her eyes and landed on the feathers. The dirt began to shimmer with a multitude of colours. Dulcinea set one feather down. Unlike before, this feather did not immediately become part of the meadow. Dulcinea took the other feather a small distance away. She set it down on the firmament of Heaven. She looked at the vast meadow she had built with the help of the Angelic Host.

She felt a twinge of sorrow as she knew she would never set foot on that heavenly meadow again. Dulcinea reached back and pulled her left wing from her back. She gasped with pain and fell to her knees. She reached back and pulled her right wing from her back. Dulcinea took her two wings and stretched them out. She laid them so that they touched the two shimmering feathers.

As the angelic wings touched the feathers, they began to arch upwards and harden. They took on the appearance of stone. It was not earthly stone for it shimmered with the colours of the rainbow due to Dulcinea's tears.

"Fear not Beloved Ones." Dulcinea spoke softly to the animals playing in the vast meadow. She watched as each animal was slowly relieved of it pain and suffering. "On the wings of angels, you shall wait without pain or discomfort for your beloved human friends. And on the wings of an angel you shall cross together into Heaven, for this is your Rainbow Bridge."

A Heavenly Gift

Antonius looked appreciatively at his tiny wooden workbench. Many millennia ago, he had carved it from a giant oak tree he had found after the Great Flood. He did not need the workbench to do his chosen task, but he found that it helped him focus. He needed that focus sometimes to help with the competing emotions of his chosen task, his True Purpose. He ran his hand over the smooth finely-grained surface and once again felt connected to the earthly world he served.

"Antonius" a small voice cried out, "Antonius."

Antonius saw the small Cherubim flying towards the area where he had positioned his workbench.

"Malachi." Antonius replied to his friend. "I cannot talk now. I have to return to Earth."

"I know." Malachi responded. "I want to come with you. I want to learn what you know and to help."

"Are you certain that this is the task you want for yourself?" Antonius asked as he gestured to his simple workbench and the tattered hem of his robe.

"You could fix your robe if you wished." Malachi answered. "Many of the other angels think it is silly to have such a tattered robe."

"It is not all joy and happiness, Malachi." Antonius stated, a slight frown creased his brow. "My task brings pain with the joy, tears with the laughter."

"But you bring the kittens to earth." Malachi

replied, "And I do love the newborn kittens."

"But I also bring the Lost Ones back to Heaven." Antonius stated.

"Please, Can I help you?"

"Yes." Antonius agreed. "You may help me."

Antonius motioned for Malachi to follow him. They walked together across the vast expanse of Heaven. Malachi noticed a simple cobblestone bridge. It shimmered with the colours of the rainbow. This side of the bridge was clear but the far side was concealed with a faint haze. Every so often, a human would appear. Sometimes they would be accompanied by a single cat or dog or bird or ferret or bunny or horse or other animal, other times they would be followed by several.

"Is that the Rainbow Bridge?" Malachi asked.

"Yes." Antonius said. "My sister, Dulcinea, built it soon after Humans befriended the first animal."

Antonius and Malachi reached a small spot where there appeared to be thousands of newborn kittens all sound asleep. Antonius walked softly amongst the sleeping kittens. He looked lovingly down upon the tiny little furry bodies.

"How do you know which ones to take?" Malachi asked.

"There are no wrong ones to take, Malachi." Antonius replied. "Each has a purpose and a destiny set for it by God. I simply place them on their path."

Antonius methodically picked from the multitude of sleeping kittens. The kittens barely stirred from their slumber as Antonius kissed them on their foreheads and placed them into the folds of his robe.

"Can I carry some?" Malachi asked.

"Certainly." Antonius replied as he picked two small Siamese kittens and placed them into Malachi's hands. "Now slip them into the folds of your robe for they get very cold."

Malachi slipped the two kittens into his robes and grinned as he felt the kittens snuggle up to the warmth of his body. Antonius smiled.

"We will go and deliver these beloved ones to Earth." Antonius said as he motioned for Malachi to follow.

Antonius and Malachi stood over the sleeping body of the pregnant Siamese cat. She was sleeping soundly and did not stir at the presence of the two angels. Antonius looked at Malachi.

"Take your kittens and give them to their mother." Antonius guided.

"But there are four within her, Antonius." Malachi asked. "Why did you have me bring only two?"

"Because that is all God said to bring."

"What about the other two?"

"They were never meant to breathe the air of Earth." Antonius said. "Do not fret for them. They will remain but a husk, an empty shell. Sometimes, that is the most merciful thing we can do."

Malachi took the two kittens from his robe and placed them next to their mother.

"Now pay attention." Antonius began to sing softly to the mother cat.

Malachi listened to the words of Antonius's song and grew sad as he heard each note and syllable leave

Antonius's tongue. The forms of the two kittens slowly merged with the mother cat. When Antonius was done, Malachi saw that the angel was crying and that his tears fell softly on the still sleeping cat.

"Why do you weep, Antonius?" Malachi asked. "Is not birth of a creature a joyous thing?"

"The creation of life is a joyous event." Antonius replied. "But life for these two will not be happy or pleasant. You wondered why we only brought two kittens. It is because the Humans who own this poor creature do not care for it properly and see it as a means to satisfy their own greed. Their callousness is why we could only bring two."

Antonius brushed the tear from his cheek.

"Come." Antonius moved away from the sleeping cat and her ready to be borne kittens. "We have many more to deliver yet."

Malachi followed Antonius to the next cat. Antonius once again pulled a certain number of kittens from the fold of his robe and placed them next the sleeping cat. Once again with his mournful song, he merged the kittens with their new mother. The act repeated itself over and over. Malachi thought his heart would break as he felt the loss Antonius carried in his song. Soon there were no more kittens in Malachi's or Antonius's robes.

"We have one more thing to do." Antonius said. "For now, we have to guide the cats and kittens who have passed back to Heaven."

Antonius took Malachi to a dreary forlorn spot. The building might have once been a warehouse where Humans worked and toiled, but now it was blackened and lifeless. Antonius moved to a small corner where several charred beams and pieces of wood had collapsed. Malachi gasped as Antonius lifted the burnt wood away and exposed the still, scarred body of a cat.

"Poor cat." Malachi mourned, "I hope she did not suffer."

"But she did." Antonius replied. "She suffered most cruelly. But she gave her life in an attempt to save those she held most dear."

Antonius gently moved the body of the cat and exposed the uncharred forms of three small kittens. Unlike their mother, their bodies bore no mark of fire.

"Knowing that she could not escape, she placed her body between her kittens and the fire in hopes of saving them with her sacrifice. But it was for naught, for although the fire did not touch them, the smoke surely did." Antonius noted. "And now it is time to take them all home."

Antonius knelt beside the still forms of the cats. He pulled one feather from his left wing and placed it on the ground in front of him. He then pulled another feather from his right wing and set it next to the other. Antonius repeated this pulling of feathers from his wings until he had four sets lying on the ground. He reached down to hem of his robe and pulled a thread from the silken cloth. Gently, he bound two feathers together with the thread and then he placed the feathers on the charred body of the mother cat. Malachi listened to Antonius as he worked on the feathers. Once again Antonius was singing, but the song was not mournful or sad. It was full of joy and happiness. Malachi was confused. Antonius placed his fingertips to his lips and then touched his hand to the feathers on top of the mother cat. There was golden shimmer as the feathers grew into a set of angel wings and attached themselves to the mother cat's back. As they grew and fixated onto the cat's body, the scars and burn marks from the fire faded. Antonius placed the feathers onto the kittens and placed a kiss onto each kitten. He sang as the wings appeared and smoke-filled lungs once again breathed clean air.

"That's why your robe is tattered." Malachi stated.

"Yes." Antonius replied. "This is why it is always tattered; never more than thumb-width, but never less. My tattered hem is a reminder of all the cats I have brought back to Heaven. To repair it would not be right."

"But why was the song placing the kittens on Earth so sad, but the song of their death so happy." Malachi asked.

"The song of their birth is sad, because I know that I might be dooming them to a life of fear, pain and loneliness far from the grace of Heaven." Antonius said. "But my joy knows no bounds when I know that I have come to return them to Heaven. I am allowed to free them from their existence on Earth and bring them back into the light of God."

"Some of the cats will choose to stay at the Rainbow Bridge and wait for the Humans that cared for them." Antonius stated. "But Lost Ones, such as these, will come back with us to Heaven, for they have no one to wait for at the Rainbow Bridge."

Antonius scooped up the three kittens and motioned for Malachi to pick up the female cat. The kittens purred and squirmed in Antonius' arms. The female cat looked over at her kittens and accepted that they were finally safe. She snuggled into Malachi's robe.

"Now we take them home." Antonius smiled to a beaming Malachi.

Malachi smiled back and then briefly closed his eyes. The hem of his robe unraveled to match Antonius's. Only a thumb-width. No more. No less.

A Shattered Heart

Antonius and Malachi delivered the last of the kittens contained within their hem-frayed robes to the softly breathing calico as she lay in her sheepskin lined bed. The young cat turned her head and regarded the two faintly glowing forms that only she could see. Antonius smiled and he placed a gentle kiss on her head.

"Sleep well, young mother." Antonius gently smoothed the fur on the young cat's head. "Your babies are safe and will be here before the morn. Raise them as you were raised. Love them as you were loved. And when it is time for them to go out amongst the world, give them the strength they will need."

The young calico blinked once and then settled her head on her paws. She could already feel the life within her stirring and longing to breathe the air of the world.

"Time to go, Malachi" Antonius' face took on a slight grim tone.

"I know, Antonius" Malachi replied, his face grew downcast. "We have brought life to those we carried and now its time to take our friends home."

"Remember." Antonius replied, "There is no greater joy than to return to the glory of heaven."

"I know." Malachi said as his little wings lifted his tiny body into the air. "But I don't seem to find the same joy as you. I don't know why. I feel joy when we bring them to Earth, but I feel sad when we return them to Heaven."

"You are attuned to the human spirit, dearest Malachi." Antonius stated. "You feel as they do. Joy at birth and Sorrow at Death."

"I wish I felt as you." Malachi stated.

"And I wish that I felt as you." Antonius smiled. "Come, we have some furriends to take home."

Malachi nodded and he followed Antonius into the ether.

Malachi looked at the final spot that Antonius lead him too. It seemed too clean and too modern by even human standards to be a place where Antonius needed to retrieve the Lonely Ones. He could hear the voices of other cats and dogs. Until now, Malachi had only followed Antonius to places where the lonely still forms of cats has laid unwanted and unclaimed in deserted and vacant spaces. This entire space felt wrong to Malachi. It felt like a place of hope but it bore the taint of desolation and loss.

"Where are we?" Malachi asked. "This place does not feel right. It feels confused; torn between hope and fear."

"That is its curse." Antonius replied. "This is an animal shelter. The humans within try to help those cats who have been abandoned by other humans, but alas, they cannot save them all."

Antonius lead Malachi to a room. Malachi's small heart nearly burst at the sight that he beheld.

There in the clean sterile room were the still forms of dozens of cats; young, old, once sick or even once healthy, were piled unceremoniously near a double steel door. The cherub had never seen this number of Lonely Ones in a single place. He could not understand how they all managed to end up here. Not one of them bore sign of trauma or injury.

"What happened?" Malachi asked.

"Apathy." Antonius replied. "Indifference, carelessness, and thoughtlessness."

"This young boy was loved briefly by a little girl." Antonius said as he lovingly picked the long furred body of a young grey male cat. "But his humans did not bother to get him changed so that he wouldn't spray as his nature said he must. In time, they blamed him for the messes he made instead of their own carelessness, ignorance and apathy. So he ended up here."

"This little girl and her four siblings." Antonius set the little grey cat down and then exposed the still forms of five older kittens. "They were born to a cat that also had not been changed. The humans did not know what to do with them so they were abandoned here in a box during the middle of the night. No one else came to claim them or to give them a Forever Home."

Malachi turned away from Antonius and wiped his eyes on his silken robe.

"Did we not know this when we brought these to Earth?" Malachi asked as he motioned towards all the still forms. "If we knew this, why did we bring them only to face this terrible, lonely end?"

"We bring them in hope that humans will do what is right." Antonius replied as he placed wings on the last still form. "We are not given to question or change what humans do on Earth. They have been given the capacity to nurture and love. We have no power to force them to heed that nature. Come, we have one more place to go."

Antonius and Malachi stood next to a dirty rusty trash container.

"We cannot be here to find Lost Ones, Antonius." Malachi cried. "Even humans cannot be this callous."

"Malachi." Antonius placed his hand on his friend's shoulder. "I am sorry that you have to see this, but to do this task, you will be forced sometimes to see the worst of the humans' handiwork. I have tried to shield you from the worst but I felt it was time for you to see everything."

Antonius lifted the lid for the dumpster. He exposed several plastic bags tossed in amongst the other human refuse. Malachi looked on as Antonius gently lifted the body of a female cat and her kittens from the garbage bag. There were no signs of trauma on the still bodies.

Malachi's wings drooped at the sight of the still forms. They were similar to the bodies he had seen in the backroom of the Shelter. Malachi tried to withhold the tears that threatened to flow down his cheeks.

"Who?" was the only word that could escape Malachi's throat.

"Humans." Antonius stated. "Humans who hide behind the ideal of Ethics and Fairness for all living creatures, but no Human who understands those two words, should ever be able to do this."

Malachi watched as Antonius attached wings to all the still forms in the dumpster. He tried to stop the tears that flowed down his cheeks. He found that he could not. As Malachi stood and stared at the still forms, he barely noticed the feathers as they fell from his wings and drifted to the ground.

"Malachi!" Antonius snapped sharply, "Mind your wings!"

"Antonius." Malachi dropped to his knees as the last feathers from his wings fell to the ground and his wings withered against his back. "My heart is broken. I have no more strength. I was wrong to think that as a cherub, I could handle your task like you."

Antonius lifted his fragile friend up from the ground.

"I will take you home." Antonius said. "I should never have let you accompany me."

"No." Malachi said softly. "I do not want to go home. Take me to the Rainbow Bridge."

Antonius took Malachi back to the earthly side of the Rainbow Bridge. There were thousands of animals playing and running in the sunlit meadow. Antonius started to set Malachi down. Malachi grabbed and held Antonius' robe tightly.

"Not here." Malachi pleaded. "Take me far enough away that I can still see the Bridge, but no one can see me."

Antonius took Malachi to the limit of human vision away from the Rainbow Bridge. He set Malachi down. Antonius fully expected Malachi's wings to grow back. Malachi stood up to his full height, which barely took him to Antonius's hip. He reached back and pulled his withered left wing from his back. He tossed it so that it was on the far side of the Rainbow Bridge as far away from the bridge as he was. Where his withered wing landed, a small cliff with two empty pools formed. Malachi took his withered right wing and he laid it down on the ground in front of him. As it touched the ground, a dry creek bed grew towards the Rainbow Bridge and the newly formed cliff and empty pools. Malachi sat down on a small rocky ledge on the Heaven side of the dry creek bed. The tears he had tried to hold in on Earth began to flow uncontrollably. Antonius watched as the creek bed began to fill, water flowed under the Rainbow Bridge and two waterfalls started to cascade over the small cliff and filled the two small pools.

"I can no longer help you Antonius." Malachi whispered through the tears that flowed down his cheeks and into the creek at his feet. "The Sense of Loss and the Memories of all those cats and kittens has shattered my heart and destroyed my wings. I am sorry that I could not bear the weight of such feelings like you. Maybe as Humans find the two Pools I have made, they will learn what a precious gift they have been given. I can only hope that they will soon realize what they squander and that they will change their ways."

Antonius left his friend's side and flew to the two pools at the base of the small waterfalls. He dipped his finger into the one pool and he felt the loss that had shattered the cherubim, Malachi's, heart. He then tasted the water from the other pool and he felt all the joyous memories that Malachi felt as he had helped Antonius bring the kittens to Earth. Antonius let a tear fall from his eye into his hand. From it, Antonius created a silver cup and a thin length of chain. Antonius fixed the chain to the first pool.

"This is the Pool of Loss." Antonius stated and then he created a second silver cup and chain from another tear. He affixed this cup to the second pool of water. "This is the Pool of Memory."

He summoned another being of Heaven and instructed it to watch over the two pools.

"These are the Pools of Loss and of Memory." Antonius instructed the creature who sat down between the two pools. "They are God's covenant to any Human that wishes to bring one of his creatures into their heart. In their dreams they shall come to this place and drink from the pools. Only those who can feel and understand what it is like to shatter an Angel's heart are worthy of such a gift."

Elbereth's Task

Elbereth stood at the threshold of the Rainbow Bridge. Across it's glimmering span, she could see her angelic sister, Dulcinea. Elbereth saw the joy in Dulcinea face as each creature crossed into Heaven accompanied by their human companion. All of the Angelic Host knew of Dulcinea's sacrifice to build this simple bridge between the earthly meadow and the vastness of heaven. Everything had a price. Dulcinea's price for the happiness and health of all the creatures that waited for their earthly friends had been her angelic wings and the ability to ever cross from Heaven to Earth. Even the meadow she had laid on angelic feathers was forever banned to her. Elbereth knew that Dulcinea drew all the joy she wanted from the knowledge that every creature that crossed the bridge had waited in peace and comfort in her meadow. Elbereth often found herself talking with Dulcinea or in the meadow amongst the multitude of creatures. She had even spent many millenniums with Antonius traveling between Heaven and Earth.

Antonius had chosen as his True Purpose to bring the souls of all the kittens to Earth and to return those who humans had abandoned or ignored to Heaven. Without forethought, Elbereth's True Purpose had become entwined with that of Antonius and Dulcinea. As she stood and watched over the Rainbow Bridge, she suddenly felt an Earthly tug at the center of her being. She nodded her head towards Dulcinea and she flew towards Earth.

Elbereth found herself hovering over two forms in a small cozy room. One form was human and one was an old frail feline. Elbereth knew why she had felt the pull to this location; a Beloved One was about to say goodbye to its human companion. Elbereth felt the sorrow radiating from the human as it patiently and lovingly waited for its feline friend to pass from the earthly world. She watched the human gently cradle the feline and lovingly stroke its fur. Elbereth felt the human's sorrow and wished it was within her True Purpose to ease its pain. Elbereth knew that she did not bring release for the human. She was here to forever bind the human to the slowly fading creature in its lap.

Elbereth watched as the feline's body shimmered. The physical body stopped as the feline's angelic form separated. Elbereth knew that the human understood that its beloved friend had finally left the Earthly Plane. It did not take angelic insight to understand the tears that coursed down the human's face. She turned her attention to the bewildered feline spirit that seemed confused and lost.

"Beloved One." Elbereth spoke to the feline spirit in its own language. "I have come to take you home."

"But I don't want to leave." the feline spirit replied. "I want to stay here with her."

"Your time on Earth has ended." Elbereth stated with a smile. "I am here to guide you to where you can wait for your friend. There you will be restored to the Beloved Friend that your human remembers. There will be no pain or sorrow for you."

"But what about my friend?" The feline asked.

"For her." Elbereth responded sadly. "There is a price."

"I will pay it." the feline said quickly. "She has given me a home and all the love I needed for the last fifteen years. Ever since I was a Kitten, I can remember feeling her love and affection."

"That is what brought me here." Elbereth said. "The Ending of a human's Earthly Love is what calls me from Heaven."

"Then what is the price she has to pay?" the feline asked.

"Watch and you shall understand." Elbereth replied.

Elbereth held an outstretched palm towards the human female. A thin silvery blue tendril began to drift from the human towards Elbereth's outstretched hand. Elbereth pulled the ethereal wisp and slowly formed a small sphere from the energy. The feline saw that a small void had formed near it's human's heart. Even the feline could sense the hollowness and pain that the void was causing the human female.

"What have you done to her?" The feline's back arched and its fur bristled. "Whatever you have done, I demand that you undo it now!"

"This is the price she must pay." Elbereth took the small sphere and laid it on the forehead of the cat.

The silvery blue energy sparked along the feline's angelic form. Elbereth smiled as the feline suddenly understood what had happened.

"For as long as this human female lives, she will feel the loss of this small piece of her essence." Elbereth explained. "In time, she will be able to bear the loss with greater ease than she does right now. But forever, she will know of its loss. In times of reflection and melancholy, she will once again feel the strength of this moment and she will remember you."

"Does it hurt her?"

"For this moment, it will feel as though her breath has been stolen from her body." Elbereth replied, "In time it will become merely an echo."

"But why."

"It may take many years for you and her to be reunited in Heaven." Elbereth stated. "Without this small piece of her essence, the two of you may never meet in the vastness of Heaven. Now you shall wait without pain or sorrow in a vast Meadow next to a Rainbow Bridge. When she crosses to Heaven in her time, you will feel her presence. You will feel the tug of her spirit and you will come running. Then you will cross the Rainbow Bridge to be together for the rest of time."

"So this is the price?" the feline asked.

"Yes." Elbereth smiled. "The pain and emptiness she feels now is to secure the eternity of happiness she wants for the two of you later. It was a contract she made the minute she decided to give you her love. In time, the void will lessen, but it will never fully heal. She may even open her heart many more times before she joins you. And each time, I will return and bind her to those she has made Beloved Ones."

"With her love." Elbereth continued, "She has asked for you to wait for her. This small pearl of her essence I have given to you is not so that she remembers you, but so that you remember her."

"I will never forget her." the feline said defiantly. "Take me to the Bridge. I am ready to wait forever for her."

Elbereth lifted the feline and placed it within the folds of her robe. She cast one more glance at the human clutching the still form of her beloved friend. Have faith, Elbereth thought as she regarded the sobbing human, One day you will be together again.

The Ones Who Came Before

Elbereth stood in the meadow next to the Rainbow Bridge and watched with a broad smile as a small band of cats chased after a ball that had been thrown by one of the many Cherubim that walked amongst the animals. The ball disappeared in a rolling tumbling mass of fur. All pain and illness had been forgotten. A small tug at her being reminded Elbereth of her True Purpose.

She walked to the Boundary of the vast heavenly meadow and prepared to cross over to Earth. She felt a strange pressure on her ankles. She looked down and saw two cats sitting primly and properly next to her on either side. One was a sleek tuxedo female and the other was a rather plump ginger male. Elbereth spoke to the two cats at her feet in the language of cats.

"What are you two doing?" Elbereth asked.

"We feel a tug." the ginger male said.

"It's more like a pull." the tuxedo female corrected.

"No." the ginger male replied. "This is definitely a tug. A pull is softer, less keen."

"I didn't like your attitude on Earth and I find it just as annoying now." The female snapped.

"No fighting is permitted here." Elbereth commanded. "Now I must go. A beloved one is about to come home."

"We know." the ginger male said sombrely. "It is my litter brother. I left him many, many years ago when we were both young."

"You know the one I go to find?" Elbereth was taken aback.

"He is tied to us as much as he is tied to the human that loved us." the tuxedo stated. "I was his foster mom when his own mom didn't want to take care of him."

"Can we come with you?" the ginger male asked. "He was always the more skittish one of the two of us. I worried about him when I had to leave,"

"It is not permitted for you to leave Heaven." Elbereth stated.

"We don't want to leave." the female said. "We want to help you bring our brother home."

Elbereth regarded the two cats sitting at her feet. What marvelous creatures God has created. You both are willing to return to the Earth to guide a beloved brother and foster-son to Heaven. Elbereth pulled two feathers from her wings. She knelt done and held the feathers out to each cat. The ginger and the tuxedo took the feathers in their mouths

"You must not lose these feathers." Elbereth warned. "Without them you will not be able to find your way back the Rainbow Bridge."

The ginger and the tuxedo nodded. They both looked up as the tug became stronger. Elbereth felt it too. She picked up the two cats and held them in her robe. The two cats held the feathers in their mouths as tightly as they could.

Elbereth was pulled to a quiet sterile room. There, sitting next to a clean white wall, were two humans stroking and nuzzling the still form of long haired ginger cat with white mitts and a thick, ruffled bib. The astral form of the cat was sitting on the floor watching its human comfort its old body.

"Hello, Beloved One." Elbereth smiled as she picked up the mitted ginger cat. "It is time for you to come home."

"But I don't want to leave." The mitted ginger cat replied. "I want to stay with them."

"Don't be scared, brother." The ginger male wiggled his way out of the folds of Elbereth's robe and talked around the feather he held in his mouth. "Where we go there is no pain or sorrow."

"My little boy, you've grown so large." The tuxedo gushed through her feather. "Elbereth is going to help our humans find us, but it's going to hurt them."

"No, please don't hurt them." The mitted ginger cried.

"It is the price." Elbereth said softly and sadly.

Elbereth reached out her hand and drew a thin tendril from each of the humans. She was shocked to find other tendrils appearing in the air in front of her. Unmistakably, these were from other humans who had felt a deep connection to the mitted ginger cat. How special of a cat to have touched so many humans so strongly. Elbereth took each wisp of energy and cast it about the mitted ginger cat. The humans clutching their beloved pet felt the hollowness form next to their hearts.

The tuxedo suddenly jumped from the folds of Elbereth's robe and walked towards the humans.

"No." Elbereth commanded. "It is not permitted."

"The humans have to know." The tuxedo replied past the feather in her mouth.

The tuxedo tried to brush her head against the female human's arm to let her that her once beloved pet was also nearby. The tuxedo's head simply passed through the human's arm. Dejected, the tuxedo brushed her head against the human male's hand, but this time the feather that allowed her to return from Heaven touched his hand. The human male gave a bit of a start as he felt something faint and soft brush against his hand.

"We are the Ones-Who-Came-Before." The tuxedo tried to explain, but the humans could not hear her. "Our brother is going to come home with us and we will wait at the Rainbow Bridge for you."

The tuxedo walked patiently back to Elbereth and stretched herself up to be picked up. Elbereth smiled as she tucked the tuxedo in next to the ginger male and the mitted ginger. Elbereth looked at the release that human male seemed to carry in his eyes. Somehow he knew they were there and that his beloved cat was in good hands.

Elbereth pulled a feather from her wing and crushed it to a fine powder in her hands. She blew the powder into the air and watched as it drifted out on unseen gusts of air.

"Now all cats will know what you have shown me, beloved Tuxedo." Elbereth said, "The knowledge of feathers is now known to all felines. As all cats grow, they will practice this and learn how to carry the feathers in their mouths. And when the time comes for them to return with me to Earth and bring their beloved friends home, they will know how to tell their humans that they are loved and safe."

Catwalk
dedicated to my Tuxedo daughter, Jasmine, and my Tuxedo nephew, Edsel the Pooch

Catwalk

On the edge of windowsill,
Clever Cat, never still.

Pours along in shimmer fur,
Touches light, liquid purr.

Can't be "kept," so far free.
That is Cat, and should be.

Laurie Jones

Craptacular…In The Literal Sense
Fi-Fi

Yesterday was … EVENTFUL.

Let me explain. It started out normally. I got up, had a nice poo, ate some crunchy goodness, got a little drink and laid back down for a nap long before the Chief Servant was out of the potty room. Not cat-tacular by any servant's stretch of the imagination, but not a half bad way to start the day.

Then my new cat toy started ringing. What is this?!?! I want to chew on it not listen to it! The CS takes it from me and starts talking to it, like there was another servant in the room. I nearly peed myself from laughter, but I have a reputation to uphold, so I acted like I was ignoring her.

A few naps later and two new servants that I have never smelled before invaded my space. Needless to say, I wasn't happy. I didn't manage any shuteye due to the incessant noise.

Because of my world domination plans, I felt it best to pay attention, in case the CS was inviting spies to nose around my quarters. So, through eavesdropping, I found out it was the manservant's mom and dad from a place called Florida. Like I care where they import them from as long as they can open a can, I am peachy... Don't get smart; I am secure in my maleness.

To make a long story short, the new woman servant took a liking to me, like that was unexpected, and began petting and cooing over me like I was a toy poodle, an infantile human or some other intolerable human pansy plaything. After a few minutes of stroking, prodding and making fun of my gorgeous facial features, I told the new woman servant that I wanted her to take her paws off me.

I guess she thought I was purring in delight of the attention. Well... I wasn't.

So the only way for me to get her to lay off the goods was to deliver a powerful punch that she would understand.

Out of curiosity, do they speak another servant language in Florida? Really, I must know. It can only aid my plans in the future.

Anyway, she wasn't getting my message. So, I did what any self-respecting cat of my stature would do in a situation like this. I deposited a good measure of Stinky Love on her shirt. The sad part is, it wasn't as stinky as I had hoped because she didn't notice at first. So, I strained another portion out along side it. It was nice and wet and smeared more than I had anticipated. I am not ashamed to say that I was pleased with myself.

Well, the second helping was all it took. She had a look of fright and the CS rescued me from her clutches and put me in my litterbox. I can say that this was a little disorienting, as I wasn't expecting the CS to move so quickly. I stepped into the little pile I left in the box. I have no shame, though. It got the point across, didn't it?

However, I was NOT expecting the manservant to pick me up and proceed to bathe me, right there in front of the world to see. How rude is that?

I was agast! Full of angst! Full of rage! But, he was gentle and he made sure that it was the temperature that pleases me.

He gave me a sweet smelling shampoo and massaged my back, head, legs and nether regions. I kept thinking to myself, this is what I deserve, minus the water. In spite of the water, I took it like a man (pardon the expression). Although, afterward, I was a little perturbed. He failed to use conditioner.

It was after this that really got my knots in a bunch.

Ok. You've seen my picture. I have a very soft flowing, long, luxurious, cream-colored coat with splashes of silver on my ears, paws and tail. When you get all those precious follicles wet, they stick together. I looked like a rat, a royal rat, but a rat none-the-less.

They took turns chuckling at me. I am not the royal jester, am I? No. I am the King! The servants are here for my enjoyment. NOT the other way around.

Oh, sad is the day when you become disappointed with your servants. It makes me feel that all the training and effort I put forth to have them do my bidding is lost.

The CS dried me off then shut me in the manservant's office. Talk about gratitude. So, I banished the imposter servants back to Florida and hope that they get a dog.

By the way, after they left the CS opened a fresh can of SG for me. She even put it in a bowl this time. She's not so bad, after all.

About Fi Fi:

Fi Fi is a male, not female, hymalayan who would kill for a new name. He enjoys Bird TV, alone time and tormenting his servant staff. Fi Fi's blog, *The Life of a Cat*, can be viewed at www.TheLifeOfACat.com.

Me and My Evil Alter Ego
Hendrix the Kitty

Hi! My name is Hendrix and I am a rescued former feral. Who knew how much my life would change when I set out hunting that cold November day in 2004.

Mommy saw my little black head in the tall grass next to the side of the road just up the street from her house on her way home from work. She pulled over and checked me out and I just lay there checking her out. Realizing she didn't have any blankets in the car (and figuring I was injured since I didn't run away) she drove quickly up the block to get my daddy and bring him back to help.

When he crouched down to check me out, I crawled into his lap. Not usual behavior for a feral but daddy has a way with kitties. Long story short, I found my family. I'll even forgive them for having my bits and pieces snipped off since they take good care of all my health problems (I'm FIV positive, have IBS, bad ears and had conjunctivitis when they found me – try giving a feral cat eye drops and pills twice a day).

None of this of course compares to their ongoing tolerance of my Evil Alter Ego Bendrix. See, I am, especially for having been outside for the first 2 (approximately) years of my life, a very well behaved kitty. I stay off the furniture I'm not allowed on (which isn't much), I sleep when my beans sleep and play with appropriate toys for kitties. But sometimes, my beans would find me in inappropriate places doing naughty things, like tipping over photo frames on top of the player piano, or scratching the back of the couch over and over again. Any area of the carpet was fair game and no amount of Feliway would keep me from zoning out and digging away.

I'd be chilling on the sofa and mommy or daddy would be petting me, and one would say, "It is hard to believe this is the same kitty that jumped up on the piano earlier and got yelled at." Or, "It is hard to believe this is the kitty who scratched me so hard last night when we were doing his ears."

I would have no recollection of these activities at all! One day when the TV was left on Channel 9, a documentary called *One Life to Live* about people in a town called "Pine Valley" came on. Suddenly, it hit me, I have an Evil Alter Ego! That is why "I" was behaving so strangely with no recollection of the event. I sighed in relief that I now knew I wasn't crazy...or was I? After all, how to control an Evil Alter Ego? I'm still working on that.

In the meantime, I have to put up with hearing how I was "scratching more than usual today" and "someone got up on the table and tried to eat my sandwich." I'll admit, he is much more a daredevil than I am. It can be fun hearing of his exploits, and I never run out of food as Bendrix happily wakes mommy and daddy up whenever my food dish of crunchies is running low at 3:00 am. We hate to see the bottom of the bowl. He is very good at demanding food and 90% of the time, I wind up reaping the rewards of his efforts with extra treats! I do however have to suffer wet furs from the squirt gun when Bendrix is discovered scratching the walls or sofas, so it all evens out. Someday I hope we can do like the people on that documentary did and "integrate" our two personalities. I think I'd feel more in control that way, and probably drier…

Hey all, Bendrix here. Evil Alter Ego my tushy. "Evil" in this situation is a relative term. After all, I'm a cat! There are things cats must have and must do to be healthy and happy. I just make sure my host personality Hendrix gets everything he needs, even when he doesn't realize he needs it.

Sure a few VET techs have been, shall we say, casualties of my dislike for cold tables and sharp pointy things, but that sign saying "Exit Only" under my tail isn't a suggestion so keep that thermometer the heck away from me! My only regret is that my zealous pursuit to keep my blood in my body where it belongs has wound up with me being gassed. The VET and mommy have decided it would be best to put me out for a while when going in for tests and stuff. On the plus side, I get to see those pink mousies and hippos in tutus while I'm out. Why they insist on singing "Don't Stop Believin" by Journey I'll never know....

Anyway, back to this "Evil" stuff. Really, I'm just behaving the way I'm supposed to. Hendrix is the weird one. Cats like heights. The player piano is the highest place in the living room. It makes sense I'd want to get up there. If the beans don't want stuff knocked over, they should remove it.

Cats don't like closed doors. If a door is closed, it stands to reason I'd try to get it open. I don't have thumbs so scratching is the best I can do. As for walls, come on kitties, back me up; "There are bugs in there. I can hear them and must dig them out for your, my beans', protection from the icky bugs. I know you can't hear or see them—that is because you are human. Trust me, they're there and someday, I'll get through that drywall and prove it."

As for the food dish nonsense, I've seen my mommy cry because she only found crumbs in the Doritos bag in the pantry. Let's not even get started on what happens when there is no chocolate in the house, or chips, or rum. Those aren't even "meal foods." Crunchies are my **meal** and after spending 2 years as a hungry feral kitty, I've earned the right to a full food dish at all times, even at 3:00 am.

Waking the beans up early on the weekends. Sigh, just because they don't have to get up for work doesn't mean my tummy just all of a sudden gets full. I want my stinky goodness at the usual time and that is that. No arguing. If you don't want a cold kitty nose in your face, just set the clock and get up. You can go back to bed after serving me, I won't need you for chin scratches for a while after eating. That is my grooming time.

So, as you can see, I'm not "Evil," I just know what I need to be happy and healthy and I'm willing to demand it! But I'll let you, the public, decide.

Visit our blog for the ongoing adventures of Hendrix the Kitty and his Evil Alter Ego Bendrix. www.mrhendrixthekitty.blogspot.com

Home

No one likes the M word which is not Meow....
The M word which means boxes and boxes
that fill with stuff and you can't play with.
Where are we going? Will I live on the streets?
Will you take me with you?
Can I take my toys?

But I love the H word, which is not Hiss...
The H word which means boxes and boxes
that empty and disappear before I can claim them.
Are we staying here? Will we move again?
Ooh, I think this is Home, cause
here are my toys!

- brandi -

OH, THE HORROR!
Bonnie Underfoot

August 29, 2007

I am REALLY hissed off. I was requesting my breakfast when that woman put the PTU[1] in the kitchen. It doesn't go there. Then, she got behind me. Of course, I growled a warning. She grabbed me and tried to shove ME into the PTU! Thats no way for a servant to treat her Queen!

Well, I nearly bit her and squirmed loose, then ran under the rocking chair. She followed, but couldn't see me. Success!

...or not. She got too close and I hissed. I couldn't help myself! This time, she grabbed me, wrapped me in a blanket and stuffed me into the carrier. I fought and growled and hissed, but this time she had me.

As I settled into one ANGRY caged cat lump, I noticed something completely insulting: The blanket is full of cat hair...VICTOR's cat hair! What NERVE that woman has, wrapping me in HIS blanket!

We spent HOURS[2] in that monster on wheels

And We Writed You This Book

and then the vet's office was full of squillions[3] of nasty DOGS! The first and smallest I could have beaten up with one paw tied behind my back. He was yapping his fool head off. Stoopid noisy dog was getting his hoohaa-ectomy! Serves him right, hurting my poor kitty ears. He'll get what's coming to him!

First she wants me in the cage, and then she wants me out. Make up your mind, Woman! Usually, I like my vet, but NOT today. I was NOT in the mood to cooperate. I hid my vein as best I could and tried not to give any blood, but she cheated and took it from my neck. Then they talked about my fur. Specifically, they pulled on the mats in my fur. THAT HURTS! And who said 'fat?' I'm NOT fat.

Well, I was carried away and left alone awhile, then the torturers got me out again and as angry as I was, somehow I fell asleep! I don't usually sleep while on guard duty! What kind of Attack Tabby would I be then?

I woke alone and caged again. Bleh! What's that nasty taste? Ow! What's in my neck? Hey! Who brushed out my mats? I didn't say you could do that! And WHO TRIMMED MY CLAWS???

After hours[4] of abandonment and neglect, someone presented my carrier. Home? Can I go home now? Really? Take me home. NOW!!!

It was only the woman, but she's an adequate chauffeur. I didn't even yell at her and maybe the blanket was a little comforting, smelling of home. My man was waiting for me with food (it's about time!) and respect.

That stoopid cowcat was still here, too. Do you know what he did? He got in my face trying to sniff me, then, of all the nerve! He PUFFED UP at me! I was only growling a little bit, sort of letting him sniff, and he got booshy!! Excuse me?

Well, I'm glad that's over with. I'm Queen of the computer room again. They say I have to go back for another "de-scaling" in a year. What do you think I am, a fish? Oh, and they have the woman putting something in my food so my joints won't ache as much[5]. Then I'll be able to groom properly and won't get matted again.

The vet confirmed once again that I'm very healthy. Oh, perhaps grumpy and difficult at times, but healthy. And about that Victor… The vet explained to my STOOPID woman that when he pokes his paw at me, he's teasing me. DUH! WHY do you think I've been so upset by it? YOU don't like to be teased, do you? I didn't think so. Now keep that food out where I can find it and leave me the HISS alone.

I'm ready for some comfort now. My charming Chase is the only one who truly understands how I feel.

Bonnie's Mom here: Bonnie had her check-up and shots, teeth cleaning, micro-chipping, and they brushed out her mats and trimmed her nails. I figured while she was "out" for the cleaning, they could get a better look at my "crabby tabby". Normally, she hisses when they look at her teeth and growls when they listen to her heart. Oh, and they didn't say she's fat; they were trying to pinch her fat layer.

[1] PTU: Prisoner Transport Unit. Cat carrier. Cage.
[2] 15 minutes, tops. We even hit every green light.
[3] Four dogs. One was panting and one was barking. Squillions: Many, many, too many to count.
[4] She was there nine hours, not even overnight.
[5] Glucosamine for cats.

brandi

Sweet lady kitty
sitting on the window sill
purring furry love

by her mama, Carol Z

What I've Learned About Life
Puff

In the almost four years I've been here on earth, I've picked up quite a lot of information, both about life in general and humans in particular. I find that they can be an interesting species and we, as cats, can provoke many interesting reactions from them.

Manners

· It's not polite to walk on your mom's toast. She'll probably yell at you and may even swat at you ineffectively. In addition, you will probably get butter or jam on your paws. If your mom's normal, she probably won't eat the toast after you've walked on it, but my mom just shrugs and eats it anyway. Further research reveals that this also applies to pita bread.

· When you cuddle your mom in bed, it's not polite to put your hiney part in your dad's face. I know this cause he keeps telling me so.

· It's never a good idea to bend your little brother. Under any circumstances. Apparently this is something of a health and safety issue.

Vomiting

Every cat vomits now and then. Let's face it; if you have fur, hairballs are part of life. Hairballs, and vomiting in general make humans squee. In fact just watching us vomit usually brings forth a whole repertoire of actions. Observe as you're trying to hock it up, your human may attempt to move you off the valuable Persian rug. Or like my mom, try to shove an old newspaper under your head. I find this to be distracting. Please, allow me to vomit in peace.

A little kitty puke is not nuclear waste. Or as "W" would say, "Kitty Puke is not nookular waste". So Mom, there is no need to don protective gear. Nor do I need to listen to your gagging theatrics while you are cleaning it up. Gee woman, I'm already embarrassed enough already!

Fun and Games

Every kitty likes fun and games, right? Here are a few special ones that I've perfected over the years.

The Kitty is *Starving to Death* Game

1. Circle around your bean and mew as if you are starving. Really ham it up.

2. Jump up on the bookcase and start knocking off the stupid tchotchkes. Don't forget to keep mewing and looking pitiful.

3. Repeat steps 1 and 2 until your dad gets up and says "This poor kitty is *starving to death*", and puts crunchies in your dish.

4. Take one crunchy and bring it into your chewed up cardboard box. Bite it in half. Eat one

half and then the other.

5. Have a nice bath as if you've just finished a huge meal. Make sure Dad sees all of this.

6. Laugh quietly as you hear Dad telling Mom, "You know what Puff just did...".

This is a really fun when you are bored in the evening!

The Shower Game

This game is particularly effective when your beans are in a rush trying to get to work. Good Clean fun! I play it with my Dad almost every morning.

Go into the bathroom with your bean and pretend you're gonna look out the window at the cat politics in the backyard. Sit there and be a good kitty for a few minutes because you really have to get your timing right.

After he shuts the door and goes into the shower, wait a couple seconds till he's good and wet. Then jump down to the door and mew as loudly as you can. It's also helpful to paw the door at this point. If you mew loud and pitiful enough, you can get your bean to try and reach out all soapy and dripping to try and open the door for you. It's a great way to start your day!

Owww, help meeeeeeeeeee!

In this game, when Mom bends over to put down our food or pick something up, I jump on her back. Sometimes I do it when she bends over the sink to brush her teeth. This morning we even played it when she was putting on her bra!

We call this game "Owww, help meeeeeeeeeeee!" for obvious reasons. Sometimes Dad even comes in to see what the fun is all about.

No Puff, no!

I play this game every time my mom sits down with her knitting. This is basically every time she sits, unless I let her use the computer. She knits a lot of different things, but she is almost always knitting socks. Here's how to play. Wait til Mom gets all comfy on the couch knitting away. Sneak up real quietly and casually. Then pick up the ball of yarn and run away real fast with it. This game is called "No Puff No", because that's what Mom likes to say when we play it. Sometimes I even run around the dining room chairs a few times because that makes it more fun for her!

Breaking Things

Now this is one activity I've turned into my own personal art form. I'm proud to say my humans insist they've never seen another cat who can break things like I can. Luckily they have been very supportive and provide me with lots of crap to knock over and send sailing toward destruction.

One of my favorite things was a jar of homemade sweet pickles I knocked off the counter in the kitchen. Boy was that ever a sticky mess of pickle juice and shards of broken glass. Of course I got banished to the basement for that one, but it was truly worth it!

My least favorite thing I broke was a creamer that Mom made in ceramics class. I felt bad about that one, but it was just sitting on the counter looking all cute and innocent. It was my duty to teach it a lesson. It's not like it was the *only* thing she ever made in ceramics, I mean she studied for a couple years. Unfortunately she never got past the stage of making little tiny things.

Sometimes I like to pretend it's all in the name of science, but really who am I kidding. Breaking things is fun! Gravity is my friend! Seriously, if the time space continuum is ever disrupted, I'll be the first one to notice gravity malfunctioning. And of course, in the interest of public service, I shall warn the masses!

In Silence...

In silence our faces meet
fur and skin cheek to cheek
nighttime kisses, hearts that sigh
shadows in moonlight
Beau Beau, Angie, and I

Brenda Bentley

My First Five Days
HRH Yao-Lin

Here we have a glimpse of the first five days of my life with my human slaves. This is disturbing reading - I would advise the more sensitive of you to turn the page now.

Day One:
Am wrenched from the palace in which I was born. Arrive in a house that can comparatively be called a hovel. Ignore the two stupid humans as they fuss and fawn over my kittenish beauty. Watch them with utter contempt for a few minutes, before hiding under the cabinet. Am too disgusted with my new abode to socialise. Cannot believe I have to live in such conditions. Wonder where my other slave/breeder is. Wonder why she betrayed me. Feel wretched, and bitter. Howl very loudly to show my displeasure. Howl some more. Am picked up and brought into the large bed in which the humans sleep. Rest under the covers, too exhausted to move. Cannot believe I have to share a bed with stinky humans. Eventually fall asleep.

Day Two:

Still disgusted with my abode. Why does a Royal Siamese Prince only have four rooms? Where are the stairs and the other slaves? Am served cat food. Cat food!! Wonder what these humans take me for. Cannot believe they have not had previous experience of servitude to a Royal Siamese. Wonder how the humans cope with day to day life as they obviously can't cook or take orders. Howl lots. Howl some more. Feel horrified as the humans serve themselves spaghetti bolognaise and neglect to serve any for me. Steal some from the male human's plate. Notice that he seems dopey and a little more stupid than the female. Laugh as he eventually tries to push me away. Steal food from the female human. Apparently she finds it cute. Realise they are both equal in stupidity. Begin to hatch a plan of escape.

Day Three:

Am served cat food (again). Pretend to be sick after sniffing it. Am served a proper cooked dinner. Feel as though I am making progress. Train the slave to play fetch with me. Listen to 'ooh's' and ahh's of delight. Look at them both with hostility. Cannot believe they have never seen a cat play fetch before. Wait until they are asleep before ignoring the scratch post in favour of the sofa. Move onto the bookshelf. Knock all the ornaments over. Feel exhausted but pleased with all of my hard work. Scratch the male slave on the face until he lifts the covers so I can sleep.

Day Four:

Am alone all day. Cannot believe I do not have a human slave at my beck and call. Look for escape route. None found. Feel angry, and bored. Amuse myself by scratching furniture, knocking over cd's, kicking litter all over the floor and strategically placing poo prints all over the counter and pillows. Manage to crawl under quilt on giant bed. Sleep. Am awoken by humans returning from work. Cannot believe they have the nerve to awaken me. Shout at them for an hour until they cook me dinner. Am served steak. Feel pleased with the menu and make mental note to refuse all other culinary offerings from now on. Bite human slave when she tries to pet me. Laugh at the expression on her face. Roll around on the floor to show cute tummy. Bite her again when she moves in for a cuddle. Laugh once more at her stupidity.

Day Five:

Am offered toys. Ignore them in favour of watching the fish tank. Am bought plush 'cat bed'. Refuse to sleep in it. Knock over guitar. Cannot believe how much noise it makes. Watch human pick it up. Knock it over again. Laugh. Learn that net curtains rip when pulled. Set about ripping them all. Have by now created small hole in the sofa. Work on making it bigger. Spot male slave eating trifle. Insist on licking some from the spoon. Human seems bemused. Realise I will have to work much harder to instil fear. Reflect on past week. Realise the humans' need me far more than I need them. Feel proud as I fully embrace the mammoth task of training these two idiots. Chuckle to self as they once again fuss and fawn over me.

So, there you have it - I hope this wasn't too upsetting. I am quite the martyr, you know. Of course, it went steadily downhill from then on, what with the hoo-ha-ectomy and the onslaught of Baby Mao. But that is another story.

Windy Day

A kitty went climbing up a tree,
Just to see what he could see.
    But it got windy
    And the branches got bendy,
So the kitty needed some help to get free.

Karen Jo Gray

What I Learned About The Early History of Northamerica
Ko Ko Schumacher

1. A squilion years ago, Asian cats came over a land bridge up near Alaska and Russia. These cats spread out and became the first tribes on the continents.

2. Around -3000 lots of feffers and bones and litter were found in caves showing the first known ancient cat boxes in the new world.

3. Around -1500 the ancient cats began growing catnip for personal use.

4. Sometime around -200 cats started using pottery bowls to hold their food.

5. In 400 ancient cats in Ohio were burying large piles of kitty toys for the future.

6. In 750 corn based crunchy-dry-crap kitty food is developed.

7. Approx. 1000, native cats begin to develop their own regional styles of decorative kitty toys.

8. At the same time, horned Nordic cats reach Canada on scary ships from a greenland. Some stayed and married into native cat tribes resulting in Maine Coon cats ancestors. At one point the horns were lost 'cause they weren't useful anymore.

9. In 1492, Chris Catlombus finds a missing island called Carrybean and gives it to the King of Spain.

10. In 1497 John Catbot sprays Newfoundland for England.

11. In 1513, Pounce de Lion discovers sunny Florida and starts a line of popular cat treats.

12. In 1620 a group of 'beans with their cats land in Cape Cod for fresh fish and religious freedom.

13. In 1683 the Quaker Oat Man starts the first schools for girls and boys and starts the day with a healthy breakfast.

14. Around the mid-1600s the first slaves are brought to America against strong advice from settler's cats about enslaving anyone.

15. In 1754 the French go to war with the Native Americans for 7 years over Canada and fishing rights.

16. In 1766 the British monarchy begins taxing kitty food.

17. In 1773, catnip turns the waters of Boston Harbor green during a nip party gone wrong.

18. In 1775 Paul Revere's cat howls into the night waking the colonists and starting a war of interdependence.

19. During 1776, patriot and cat owner Tho-

mas Jefferson commits plagerism when he runs out of ideas while writing the Declaration of Independence for his many fathers.

20. In 1789 the Constitution of the United States is adopted removing all rights from native cats, but setting up a government of checking balances that puts the new country into immediate debt.

21. In 1789, George Washington becomes the first neutered president of the USA after his cat steals his wooden teeth.

22. During 1791 the Bill of Rights takes the first baby steps towards what will later grant equality to many American animals after the founding father's cats break into the drafting room at night add the words "free", "freedom", "not infringe", and various other additions.

23. The United States continues to grow and take over the territory of Native Americans who had first pooping rights. They also tromp on Mexicans to the south, claiming their litter box for themselves.

24. In 1865, as the nation finds some 'beans are getting smart about not owning other 'beans, the country goes to war and sales for blue or gray cat collars skyrocket.

25. 1914-1919 The Great War involving many countries and species.

26. Bad kharma and economic policies leads to a great crash in 1929 after money falls down onto the heads of wall street and becomes useless in the resulting trample.

26. 1939-World unrests and the final breakdown of the balance beam of power in Europe drags

everyone back into a war resulting in more deaths than any cat fight previously.

27. In 1941, America comes late to the fight after being smashed and foot kicked in Pearl Harbor. The entrance of our soldiers gives the allies enough strength to beat the enemies of freedom and democatcy.

28. The mid-1950 era sees the arrival of a cold war, a beginning of civil rights, and a huge burst in 'bean litters.

29. 1960 sees the beginning of the catnip culture, the beatniks, and many many long nip induced trips and catnaps. 'Beans finally realize the cat wisdom of free sex, love, and good howling music. Unfortunately this doesn't last.

30. Once again, the economy dumps a poop on the floor instead of the litter box in the 1970s and tension mounts with the prices of cat food.

31. Some kind of pendulum swings back and forth dying to be chased and the 1980s see a growth in the kitty, then a culture of bad clothes and waste takes over.

32. In 1989, beings in Berlin finally realize that there is no wall that can keep cats inside. Cats mark the wall before it comes down and this symbolizes the end of the cold war.

That's as far as I got.

Wendell's Food Haikus
Wendell Entin

If I cry enough
She'll give me some people food
That is why I'm fat.

Macaroni, Cheese
Not cat food, but a cat's food
This cat's, anyway

Once I ate plastic
Five thousand dollars later
It was out of me

"Newman's own," she says
"It's human-grade food for cats."
Fine. Let HER eat it.

Sometimes I eat corn.
I know it's not normal but
I love my niblets.

You know what tastes good?
Bacon. And sardines. And shrimp.
. . . What the human has.

It's true what they say
My breathe does smell like cat food
You expect roses?

Wake the human up
Slap her in the face with paw
I don't eat alone

Refrigerator
That's what it's called, I am told
How to open it?

Gimme some turkey
Don't slip in any dark meat
Cat don't eat that junk

I won't take my pill
Even if it's bacon wrapped
I'll take the bacon

Lick the food before
The human can eat it and
It is all yours, cat.

DISCOVER
Dee Francis

A discovery was made on a whim while I was reading the daily comics on the internet a few years ago. At the bottom of strips are various hypertext links. Normally, I would just ignore the advertisements and links on a website. My interest is in the page's main content; not in making online purchases.

At the bottom of one strip, I believe it was "Get Fuzzy" by Darby Conley, there was a link to 'Max, the Psychokitty' (http://psychokitty.blogspot.com). Being a cat lover and owner I wondered what a psychokitty was.

My own cats act up now and then: running through the house at all hours of the day (and night) chasing nothing I can see. Jumping up on the furniture and off. They sometimes don't like being picked up to be hugged or petted. They squirm madly in my arms to be let down. What wild behaviors did Max do to deserve the psychokitty nickname. Or, was it his owner the one that was pyscho, mistaking normal feline behavior?

I took a chance and clicked on the link. Max's

webpage soon appeared on the screen. The page was a blog. A blog can be thought of as an online diary posted for anyone to read. An interesting fact is that on some blogs the reader may leave a comment (which is also public and can be read by anyone). This allows the readers to interact with the blog's author Some sites do not allow comments except from other bloggers or not at all. (To limit the spam—unwanted email—that the blog's owner receives.) Sometimes, the comments may be more interesting than the subject of the original post.

I was expecting a page where some cat owner was writing about how weird and wild their cat was acting. What I found was a post, supposedly written by Max, a cat, complaining about how his owners were late serving him his dinner. How he was threatening to poop on their pillows to show his displeasure for having to be made to wait for his dinner. Or that he would put the bite on some of the people's things. Or when he did get his dinner, (a can of wet cat food), how there was not enough of it. How very important it was to feed the kitty on time—that it was the people's only job.

I remembered the old saying: Dogs have owners, Cats have staff. Max was certainly expressing that viewpoint. I laughed very hard while reading the post. It was the manner that he wrote about his annoyance that was so amusing. I could almost believe that a cat had actually written the entry.

Max's webpage is a small part of the internet that is known to its fans as the cat blogosphere. I still visit Max's site when I get on the internet. Some-

And We Writed You This Book

times he's humorous, sometimes serious, sometimes in between the two; but, he always has an opinion.

There are other pages of the cat blogsphere that one can visit. Max's site has links to other cat blogs listed on his page. Some have become regular reading for me. I try to visit each site when possible; but, there are quite a few! It would take most of the day to visit them all. Keeping up to date is not too difficult as only a few bloggers post a new entry every day.

Some of these sites are supposedly written by the kitty and has the kitty's point of view. Others are from the viewpoint of the cat's staff. All describe what is happening in the feline's world: what they may be eating, how well they are behaving, where they may be going, or how their health is. Their posts may be humorous, or serious.

Most bloggers have more than one cat in their household. Occasionally, there is a post about these other cats. Some of these other cats may have their own website.

I envy these writers their imagination and creativity. Their stories are quite convincing. You would actually believe that a cat did write the entries on those blogs allegedly written by the kitty.

(Sorry Max. While cats are pretty smart, I have yet to see one type a coherent sentence—much less write one out longhand with pencil and paper!)

I also thank them for their willingness to share the lives of their kitties and sometimes themselves on a such a public forum as the internet. It is very obvious that they love their feline friends very much. They and their kitties are like old friends and family: I care about how and what they are doing.

Also obvious is that they care about each other. These cat bloggers seem to have formed a close and caring community on the internet. When one of them is having problems the others will tell how they may have solved a similar problem. Often the advice given is quite practical. Some have even donated money to help.

Should one of other bloggers be ill, the others will leave a comment wishing them a speedy recovery. They may tell how they were treated for the same illness. They may suggest ideas on how to make the ill one feel more comfortable.

During the tainted pet food episode last spring (2007) almost all the cat blogs had warnings on them. They linked to sites that had lists of which foods were possibly tainted with the poison. Which foods had been recalled by their manufacturers. What actions the Food and Drug Administration were taking to detect and protect the pet food supply.

If one of the blogging kitties should die, the others will be there to try to comfort and console the late kittie's people. They understand what it is to lose a loved and valued member of the family. There are often moving tributes to the late feline.

As to why Max is called the Psychokitty, I'm still wondering. As well as how Edsel the Pooch, and Mouse got their names. Yes, they are cats—not a canine or rodent! If you don't believe me, get online and check out their websites, along with the others of the cat blogosphere.

1,018
Is My Lucky Number
Perfectly Parker

I guess the beginning is always a great place to start. My name is Parker. I am a cat. I think I am about 6 years old. I don't know when my birthday is because I had no home when I was born. I was what you would call a feral cat. The best guess for my birthday? Sometime in August back in 2001. But I want to tell you how I know my lucky number.

The place where I was born is called Southwest Kansas. It is very rugged country with many animals that think cats make great appetizers. I had to be very cautious outside. There were big noisy trucks and cars and the weather could be freezing and very hot all in the same day. Any food I ate I had to catch myself or get out of garbage dumpsters. All in all it was a lousy existence and I was sad, scared and miserable all of the time. Most of my days were spent under a tool shed by an alley behind an apartment building.

One day I was in the alley, slinking down the dirt road. All of I sudden I heard a human voice.

Back then I thought that humans were scary and something to be avoided at all costs. I cut across the alley as quickly as I could and hid under my tool shed. I did not know it at the time, but that voice was the voice of my Daddy. He saw me slinking down the alley and thought I looked like a good kitty! Me! Even though I was skinny, dirty and not very friendly at all. Another thing I did not know was that he had a plan, a plan to make me a part of his family. At that time I had no idea what a family was, I assumed that the life I knew was what life was. I continued to watch this human from a distance. If he caught sight of me he would always try to talk to me. He would say things like "what a pretty kitty, here kitty, kitty, kitty." Not very original, but he would say it in a very soft soothing voice. It was OK to hear and at times I actually would stop dead in my slink and look at him. I guess that was all the encouragement he needed.

It was getting a lot colder at night and to make matters worse, I had hooked up with a male cat that promised to take care of me. I imagine you can guess how that turned out. The human that was to become my Daddy had started leaving dry food on his porch and I have to admit with the cold and no home and having kittens growing inside of me, I ate it. He would always put more out. Soon I started hanging around under his porch, but I wouldn't go anywhere near him. As time went by there was a box on his porch with towels in it. I wasn't too keen about getting in that box and it just sat there for a long time. I started to look forward to hearing his voice.

It was very soothing and I started to think of this human as not a bad thing. I let him get so close to me that he could almost touch me, but not quite. This went on for weeks and weeks. Patience is something that this guy had a lot of.

One evening it was raining very hard. I was sitting under the porch when he came home. He started to talk to me and had some food in a bowl that smelled very good. I had to find out what was in that bowl so I came up to him on the porch. He sat the bowl down. I walked to the bowl and sniffed. It smelled sooooo good! I started to eat and eat and eat. That's when it happened. I let him pet me! It felt great! This guy was OK! When the delicious food was all gone I ran away again. This became a routine for about a week, I would eat, he would pet, and I would run away. My belly was getting very big and he thought it was because I had been eating so much. Silly human!

After that week of great eating, I disappeared. The man that was to become my Daddy was very worried. He thought something had happened to me. Well, I guess he was right, something had happened to me, I became a mother of five kittens. I went back to my old hiding spot and had them there. I stayed away from him for a month. The man was very sad and thought he would never see me again. He called out for me every day, I could hear him, but I had my paws full with my babies. It was very cold outside and the longer I took care of these babies, I worried they might freeze to death. I thought about the man and I thought about the box I wouldn't go in and I thought about that great food. I made a choice to totally trust the man with me and my babies' lives. One by one I took my kittens to the box on the porch. The man could not believe his eyes; he didn't even know I was pregnant. Once I had all of them there the man gave me more of that wonderful food and I ate two bowls of it. I stayed in the box on the porch that night with my babies. It was pretty nice since my belly was full and there was shelter against the wind and the cold. I thought I had made a good decision.

The next day the man left, he was gone a long time, but when he came back he had a lot of things that he took into his apartment. I stayed in the box with my kittens and watched him. After he took everything in the house he propped open the door to his apartment and put a bowl of that wonderful food right inside of the apartment. I just couldn't help myself; I had to eat some more of that food. I went in the apartment - I was nervous, but I was hungry! I ate the bowl of food and ran back out to the kittens. The man left the door open while I was back on the porch, but he had put a litter box, a big soft kitty bed, toys and some kitty treats out where I could see them inside. It took about 2 hours, but I came back inside and looked around. So this was a home! It looked very nice! The man gave me some pets and fed me some treats and talked very soft to me. That was all it took. I had made my little kitty mind up. It was a good place to be and I wanted to be with this man. I went out on the porch and one by one, carried my kittens in the apartment. I was home! I'm very smart and I knew what the litter box was for. My kittens were having a good time with the toys but they were scared of the man at first. It took a long time for them to let him play with them and give them pets.

I could have stayed like that for the rest of my life and have been very content. Shortly after we moved in with the man he took us to a place where they made us all fall asleep and when we woke up I had a sore belly. All of my kittens had boo-boos too! The man said that it was so none of us could make any babies again. I was OK with that, just give me some more food! The kittens were getting to be pretty independent and the man found homes for all of them! One by one we said our good byes until I was the only kitty left in the apartment. My life seemed very good, the man was kind and he taught me that humans could be good. Every week he would leave for a few days and someone else would come and visit me while he was gone to feed me and spend time with me. I missed the man, but I still didn't have a lot to complain about.

Some of you might be wondering if I missed being outside. The short answer is no. Once I came in the apartment I never, ever tried to get outside again. I had so much pain and trouble out there, I really did not miss it. I could look out the windows and see the birds and the sky and the grass and I still could take naps in the sun. But by being inside, I never had to worry if I was going to get attacked by a dog or a coyote or another cat! I'm not stupid, inside is waaaaaay better than outside. I highly recommend it to all kitties!

When the man would come back from being away he would always bring different smells with him. I thought I could smell other kitties and I even thought I could smell a dog. This troubled me because I had come to think of the man as my very own. I wondered where he went and why he smelled of other furs and places. I would soon find out. I was ready to discover part of my lucky number.

The day that my world changed again was very cold. The man had his big black bag out and I knew he would be leaving for a few days. Next to his bag was another boxy thing that had a fluffy towel placed in it with a few of my toys. I am curious by nature and I stepped in the boxy thing to investigate. THE MAN SHUT THE DOOR AND TRAPPED ME! I screamed, I howled, I cried, I meowed for all I was worth! Nothing I did worked. He kept talking to me in a soft voice and TOOK ME OUTSIDE AND PUT ME IN THE BIG NOISY MACHINE! This made me think he was going to abandon me and I would be homeless again. It made me very sad to think that he would do that so I just curled up in a ball and cried and cried and cried. The man told the woman that I came to know as Mommy that I cried for 220 miles and that he thought I might have broken my meower. I fell asleep from exhaustion and 163 miles later we were in a new city and a new state. There was a big house that I was carried in to with a new person. She followed the man and me into a big room that had my food and my litter box. How did they get there? Even my toys were there! My bed from the old place was there with my smells on them. There were other towels in the room as well. They had other kitty smells on them. After I was released from my box I slunk around the big room and smelled everything. The man and the woman sat on the floor while I investigated. I would not go near the woman. I let the man touch me and he spoke softly and explained that this was my new home and that I would live with him and the woman and the other kitties and a dog. OTHER KITTIES?!? A DOG!?! There were other kitties and a dog here??? I thought about escaping. I wondered where I was. It was a lot noisier here than at the old place and I knew I would never find my way back to the old apartment. I didn't know what to do and I was tired and I was hungry and I needed to use my litter box. So I decided to rest up and devise a plan to escape when I woke up. I kept thinking that I would devise a plan to escape, but every day I would eat and nap and play and spend time with the man and the woman. Once in a while I would see another kitty paw under the door and it would smell like the towels in my room. I could hear the dog walk by and that made me very nervous. I was starting to think that maybe this place was OK. It had big windows and lots of room and good sunny spots to nap.

One morning I woke up to the sound of the door being opened by the man and the woman. The woman had become my friend. I liked her, she would pet me and feed me treats and even held me like a baby – I kind of liked that! When they came in the room the woman was holding another kitty. The man walked over to me and sat down and tried to pet me while the woman sat the other kitty down. It was my new sister Puff. I gotta' tell you it was not love at first sight! There was hissing and a few insults were hurled and then she left. I hid behind the man who I now thought of as Daddy. He told me it would be OK and that these things take time. He was right, to this day I tolerate my sisters and brothers, but there isn't a lot of cuddling between us. We respect each others' space and we rarely fight, but we don't spend a lot of time giving each other baths if you know what I mean.

    The introductions continued and I perfected my "Paw of Death" with the dog. The "Paw of Death" is simple. If the dog gets too close, raise your paw and give a warning meow. If the dog doesn't move fast enough for your liking – BAP, right on the snout! It's a very effective tool and I highly recommend it. Oh, I forgot to tell you, never use your claws, it's considered rude by the humans.

    Life in the big house in the big city was good. There was always someone around to attend to my every need. Food was plentiful and the windows were big. I had lots of nappy spots and a porch that was screened in where I could catch a breeze and watch the local wildlife. I thought that house was where I would spend the rest of my life. Never assume kitties, never assume! I lived in that house for 5 human years. That's 5 Christmas trees I have climbed and countless fires I have enjoyed by the fireplace, thousands of naps on Daddy's lap and many other wonderful memories. A few months ago everything changed.

The woman (who I now consider to be Mommy) took a new job. When I found out, I thought to myself, "so what, as long as it buys the cat food." What I did not realize was that this new job was in a place called O Hi O. 598 miles from our great house in Missouri! I was going to have to move again! Moving is no fun. Moving is hard. Moving is stressful. I don't like to move. I am a cat and I like routine. I do not like strange people coming in the house and taking away all of our stuff. I don't like taking kitty tranquilizers and waking up in the boxy thing with no way of escaping. I really don't like doing any of this in the middle of summer. Do you know many times you get shoved around in the big metal monster when the sun shifts positions? Trust me kitties, moving is bad. But once you are settled again? It's pretty OK. I now live in O Hi O, we are all together and our new home is very nice.

I came from very humble beginnings. I know what it is like to be hungry, cold, hot, scared, sad and hopeless. I also know what it is like to have plenty of food, love, shelter and contentment. I know I am luckier than many kitties in this world.

To all you humans out there who have helped kitties in need I send you smooches and all my thanks. There is a special place in heaven for humans who show kindness and compassion to animals. I wish there were more of you around.

1,081 is the number of miles from where I started life to where I am now. 1,081 is my lucky number.

Reeport of Findings on Reserch into Gravity Free Zones

submitted by
Dr. Buddy Longwhiskers

Purrliminary reeport first published on http://2carolinacats.blogspot.com Jan. 16, 2007

With submissions of additional data from Pearl C. Pritchard; Midnight; Jeter Harris & Mickey Mantle; Rocky; Charcoalie; Fat Eric; Eric & Flynn; Alexi; Pepi; Zippy, Sadie & Speedy; Diamond Emerald-Eyes; Gemini & Cheysuli; Mr. Hendrix; Max and Black Cat.

As efurry cat knows, the world is filled wif Gravity Free Zones – areas where inanimate objeks will float wifowt falling to the grownd and cats can fly. I have dedicated menny of my waking hours to the pursoot of the Gravity Free Zone (GFZ). When I posted my first reepurrt on my blog, I was furry happy to lern that other cats were purrsuing the same reserch!

And We Writed You This Book 85

With there encurrijemint, I deesided to not only continyoo my reserch, but ekspand it and invite other cats to share there reesults as well. In this way, we hope to reach as menny cats as pawsible wif owr reesults and also collect more data to share.

As you'll see, many of the ekspurriments (inklooding mine) have focussed on dropping objekts from elevated lokashuns to see if they resist gravity, thereby defining the Gravity Free Zone and, most impawtantly, its boundries. In addition, several intrepid scientists are focussing there reserch on attemts to fly. This has resulted in impawtent data being collected regarding the ability of cats to fly. Furry eksiting data, indeed!!

Following are the purrliminary results from my and my fellow scientists' ekspurriments and reserch as we attempt to locate and label the GFZs in the Cat Blogosphere.

Ekspurriment Series 1 – Objekts dropped or pooshed from locations more than 5 cats high.

These ekspurriments consist of the scientist jumping (or flying) to the top of a purrticularly high surface, carefully moving the objekts located there to the edje, and pooshing them ofur. This is followed kwikly by observation of the item(s) to see if they float in the GFZ, or if they clonk onto the flore or efen brake into many peeses.

My own werk in this area is currently focussed on finding the GFZ in my Ant Ree's howse. I'm sure it is in my mom's sleepy room, but wen I begin my reserch at dawn, mom bean is almost allways awakened by my ekspurriments. She then interfeers by making me have snuggles in bed!

Miss Pearl C. Pritchard notes that this is furry effective "when you want the humans to get up and feed you!"

Jeter Harris reepurrts that efurry nite his human dad puts the lamp, telefone and pikshurz that are ushully on the table beeside the bed, onto the flore so that his brofur Mickey Mantle cannot check to see if there is a GFZ in the room. This seems to indicate that the human beans are aware that Gravity Free Zones exist and they are attempting to thwart owr reserch.

Charcoalie, Squillion furiend of Bonnie Underfoot and Victor Tabbycat, tells us that Victor is hard at work checking for GFZs on his mom's dresser. Unfortunately, he is having the same reesults that I am – being yelled at by the bean and chased off the ekspurriment platform. Victor is continyooing his reserch, but has moved his focus to bathroom cownters. His hypothesis is that there is a correlation between GFZs and bathroom cownters. We wish him the best of luck and look forward to his future repurrts.

Charcoalie also notes that Bonnie and Victor's mom bean beleeves there are areas of increased gravity that pull previously elevated things to the floor. For a bean, she has a purromising intellect and we hope that Victor will snoopervise any eksperiments that she may attempt.

Midnight (of Grr, Midnight & Cocoa) gives us an interrim reepurrt that the GFZ in there howse is not located near the tall bookcase in the living room, nor the shelves attached to the opposite wall. Keep looking, Midnight!

Alexi checks in with the eksiting reepurrt that there are TWO Gravity Free Zones at the Krasota Castle! They are located between the flore and the top of the beans' dresser mirrir and from the flore to the shower curtin.

Diamond Emerald-Eyes reepurrts that she has checked the kitchen and bedroom at her howse wif no luck and she will continyoo her reserch, focussing next on the bafroom.

Ekspurriment Series 2 – Attemts to fly using Gravity Free Zones

This set of ekspurriments involves the scientist leaping from one surface to another, crossing great distances wifowt falling to the flore or grownd. I have only made a few ekspurriments in this feeld, wif the unfortunate reesult that I ended up hanging off a screen dore. On the pawsitive side, I was abowt 10 cats off the grownd!

Eric and Flynn have discuvvered a parshul GFZ between the sofa and the cat tree by the window. They further note, "It helps when the skrirell looks in the window, I fink I reely fly. Of course Eric's eggstra weight stops him furrom gitting the same effect."

Pepi of the Hot(M)BC reepurrts that his "favorite GFZ is between the sofa and my glass top hangout in the living room. Amazing how I don't fall down there."

Zippy, Sadie and Speedy have discovered several GFZ's in there house..."Sadie found one between da couch and da side window and another between the side window and the end table. Zippy found one between the bed and desk and another between the bed and the dresser and I found one by da kitchen table...but if mom moves da chair over it disappears!" Another finding is that "most of dem is atween one piece of furntchur and another and seem to only work when we jump from one spot to anuffer. If we try to step between them then the gravity kicks in and we fall!"

Rocky from Artsy Catsy posts that he wishes they could get free of gravity, but is conserned that he is too fat. This seems to be a recurring theme amongst our scientists, espeshly those who are werking in pares or groops. Fat Eric also menshuns that purrhaps some cats are more aerodynamic than others, wich may be helpful in flying throo the GFZ, altho Gemini and Cheysuli hypothesize that the amownt of furrs a cat has may be a factor in the flying. The Crew's Max reepurrts that his mom bean has been insulting him regarding his wate, and he wonders if this has something to do wif his inability to bank off walls like he used to.

Miscellaneous findings and intristing reesults from eether Series 1 or Seeries 2 ekspurriments or a combinashun of bofe!

Midnite & Stray Kitty were onse agane thwarted by there mom bean wen they attempted ekspurriments. Yelling of "Get Down" and "Stop that" caused the scientists to lose there consentration and abandon there werk.

Mr. Hendrix has the following furry

And We Writed You This Book 89

provokative theories to consider. "I have found that I am much slower when getting up on high objects especially those I'm not supposed to be up on. Now, the things that I bump into seem to fall to the floor much faster than I can jump to the floor. Especially with breakables. I weigh 12.5 lbs. My speed in getting down depends on if I am getting down because I'm ready, or if mommy or daddy is coming to get me down while yelling. I'm faster then. I think it is the wind velocity from their yelling that speeds my descent."

Black Cat has an alarming reepurrt! "I haven't noticed any Gravity-Free Zones in my house (unfortunately because I am constantly dropping things and spilling liquids) but there is definitely at least one Black Hole here where stuff vanishes, often never to be seen again..."

In conclooshun, I beleeve it is obvious that further reserch is needed to proove the eggsistence of the Gravity Free Zone. Also, we must beegin more widespred investigashun into the Black Hole theery, as well as the pawsibility of Increased Gravity Zones.

I encurrage all cats to take part in these impawtent ekspurriments and be purrsistent! For some reezon, the beans don't want us to find the Gravity Free Zones!

You can keep up wif owr findings on Dr. Buddy's blog, fownd at http://2carolinacats.blogspot.com. You are allso wellcome to submit yore findings to Dr-Buddy@hotmail.com for inclusion in future reepurrts.

LC, Mighty Hunter
LC

Ooh a pom-pom… I love those. They are like mousies!! The Big Thing tosses one to me and I beat it alla round the room. When I knock one outa reach, he tosses another. I beat that one alla round the room.

I am into high FRAP. The pom-poms are now real mousies, an I hafta kill them all. Another! I catch it without trouble and pull it into me. It can't escape. HA, ha, I have it, it can't escape. I get it between my teefs an I twist aroun wif my front paws grabbin it then the back ones clawin it apart, and hop up on the big softy chair wif it. It can't get away now. I tear in circles aroun it aroun the easy chair an around in terrible fast an it doesn't know which way to escape, I pounce an I pounce an I pounce. It is so bad hurt an safe to put the bitey on and grab an sniff an lick again.

The poor mousie has no idea which way to run an it jus freezes in defeat. I whap it an carry it offa the big chair an back onna the big chair. I throw it offa the chair to the ground an when it moves again I pounce it from above. I am master, I am in control.

I have beaten it taken it over so completely. It has no idea what is up down or holewards. I take it from one room to another. It is all mine, LOLOLOL!

In the food room, I start to really chomp on it slicing it's furry sides apart to get at the goodness. But wait, there is no goodness to taste, The Big Thing is jumping up and Skeeter is staring at me. Somethin is all horrible. The mousie tastes like carpet. The Big Thing is yellin "NO" and Skeeter is turnin his head away in embarrasmint. I swallow it anyhowzits...

The Big Thing shows me what I just ate. It's a pom-pom...

Oh mouse-droppin's, I dont believe I got so excited I ate a TOY! I just eated a pom-pom. I got too 'cited!

Hey. Let me out, I need to shove a froggie down my throat to push the pom-pom out! Please? Meow, meow? MREOR, HISS!

OK, fine, don't blame me where you find it tomorrow!

ME AND MY KITTY CATS
Dee Francis

Me and my kitty cats.
Play during the day,
Play through the night.

Me and my kitty cats.
We always have fun,
Never fight.

Me and my kitty cats.
Have no worries,
Have few cares.

Me and my kitty cats.
I love them.
They love me.

Me and and my kitty cats
Are best friends for life.
As it was meant to be.

Skeeter Says:

A challenge to fill in the last lines...

There once was a Ginger from Cankyta
Who loved to sleep unner the blankyta.
He'd sleep by the knees
And keep his own fleas,
xxxxxxxxxxxxxxxx

A lovely young Tuxie from Mince
Desired to find a Tom Prince.
She groomed and she purred
And she purred and she groomed
xxxxxxxxxxxxxxx

This tabby from inside the house
Went out after seeking a mouse.
She leaf-litter pawed
And even guffawed,
xxxxxxxxxxxxxxxx

We Are Still The Kitties...

The terrible twosome, the kits
Had some sticky-seed-tails giving fits.
When their grooming tries fail
From their heads to their tail,
xxxxxxxxxxxxxxxxx

When We mouse-hunters say with a twist,
"Well, you know, it is all in the wrist",
That we may not deny
When we say eye to eye,
xxxxxxxxxxxxxxxxxx

A very bright Tabby named Watsom
Had brilliant ideas that were awesom.
But Calico Sherlock
Had some that morelike
xxxxxxxxxxxxxxxx

A seal-colored kitty, a Meezer
Attempted to pounce on a geezer.
She fell to the floor
Expecting some more,
Xxxxxxxxxxxxxxxx

By Skeeter

Want to fill in the last lines? Visit Skeeter & LC at http://skeeterandlc.blogspot.com/ and drop them...a line.

Of Memory and Loss
C.D. Smith

Before I went to sleep, I decided that the next morning I would go and get a pet. I was not sure if it would be a dog or cat or bird or something else. All I knew was that I needed, no, wanted to share my life with another creature that would accept my friendship and affection.

As I slept, I fell into a deep dream.

There before me sat the most beautiful creature, neither male nor female. To either side of this wonderous creature, there were two indentical waterfalls with deep clear pools at their base. From each waterfall, the most crystal blue water cascaded down. I was entranced. Never before had I seen seen such beauty, such serenity.

Wordlessly, the creature motioned for me to come towards the pools at the base of the waterfalls. I noticed that at each pool, there was a small silver cup attached to a fine silver chain.

"Dip thy finger into the pool and taste." the creature said as it gestured to the pool to its left.

I did as instructed. As the clear cool liquid touched my tongue, my stomach clenched with pain and my heart pounded fiercely within my chest. A hollowness rang throughout my being that I feared I would never recover from.

"This is the Pool of Loss." the creature said and then it motioned to the other pool of water. "Dip thy finger into the pool and taste."

Warily, I drew my forefinger through the water of the other pool of water. As my finger touched my tongue, a joy so deep and pure touched my soul. A wave of happiness and wonder drowned the pangs of sorrow and loss the first pool had caused.

"This is the Pool of Memory." the creature said. "If you take one of God's creatures into your heart, you must be prepared to drink from both pools. Do you accept this as your covenant, your bond with one of God's creatures?"

Silently I nodded yes.

"Then drink from each pool." The creature instructed as it motioned towards the silver cups at the sides of the pools."For now they will bear no taste, but in time you will discover how much you have partaken of each."

The very next day, I went and found a kitten at a local shelter. It was the smallest one of the litter and it was the one who seemed to need me the most.

I watched it grow and play and I revelled in the smallest joy it brought to me. But then without warning, it was taken from me in a way most sudden and cruel.

Once again I felt the pangs I had felt in my dream when I tasted the waters of the Pool of Loss. Only this time, I thought the pain would never leave.

Then, I remembered the taste of the waters from the Pool of Memory. Slowly the pain of Loss began to subside, and was replaced with the joy of Memory.

I realized that I had drank more from the Pool of Loss than the Pool of Memory in my dream. But now I knew that the Pool of Memory brought more than enough comfort to offset the pain the Pool of Loss could cause.

I now bear the knowledge that each time I open my heart to one of God's creatures, I drink from the Pool of Memory and the Pool of Loss. How much I partake depends on each creature and that, in the end, the power of Memory is so much more powerful than the power of Loss.

Winter

Large white flakes fall gently from the sky,
The ground below a blanket of white.
Eager, large yellow eyes stare
Trapped with owner behind clear glass.
'Til morning must dear kitty wait,
For snow is cold and the world is great.
A single day will not matter;
You can sleep, listening to the quiet pitter-patter.

Jessica Forward

Aliens
Sammy Meezer

There are ALIENS in our back yard.
Really.
An alien lives in the house behind us!
This is what I have observed from several hours of alien watching.

- It comes out several times a day and runs back and forth, and jumps up and down.
- Then it disappears into the closed off patio behind it's house.
- It's building another space ship.
- It wears a big box on its neck and when it runs too far it yelps.
- It never freaking stops moving.
- It has made crop circles in the lawn.
- Its pee is toxic and has killed all of the plants within a 10 foot radius.
- It makes the most bast-awful sounds when it's running around.
- When it stands up straight it's taller than my mommy!!

- My mommy akshually TOUCHED it.
- It is holding 2 kitties, 2 adult beans and a kid-bean hostage. I think it's going to eat them.
- There is also an alien across the street. It comes over several times a day to have alien conferences in the closed off patio. This alien is a midget and it is so black that it cannot be seen at night. That's its cam-o-flaj
- Mommy says that the alien that lives behind us is a woofie.
- That's just a lie.
- Woofies don't have heads as big as that and woofies are NOT taller than my mommy.
- Mommy also says it's a GIRL. HA. Girls have soft high voices. This girl alien has a really deep loud voice.
- Mommy says its name is Duh-chess. It's pretending to be royalty to fool everyone.

But I'm smarter than that.

Haiku For You
Colette Werner

Springtime is here now-
The birds fly past my window
I chitter at them.

I own my humans-
But they think that they own me.
I let them think that.

Snow falls from the sky;
I stand on the porch and hiss.
It invades my space.

Mating season now,
I used to have some kittens.
My humans spayed me.

Birds sit on the tree;
They see I can't get to them.
They know they taunt me.

And We Writed You This Book

Red dot on the floor
How I love but yet hate thee.
I chase but can't catch.

Ball rolls on the floor,
I run and chase and bat it.
It's filled with cat crack.

Mousie runs away
It comes inside when its cold.
I want to catch it.

I see other cats.
I hiss and growl then chase them.
They get scared and run.

I rub on humans
Just to get them to pet me.
It makes me purr lots.

I don't have to work.
Humans give me all I need.
Being a cat rules.

Kitty friends are gone
They are at the Rainbow Bridge.
We'll see them again.

Bugs fly all around.
Springtime brings them out to play.
They make good presents.

I clean my whiskers
After eating my cat food.
Damn it tasted good.

I lay on the bed-
Sleeping next to my human.
I dream of the birds.

If you're mean to me
I will poop on your pillow.
So says the Great Max.

I am out of food
I yowl and you come running.
I love my servants.

I will glare at you
If you don't do what I want.
That will sure teach you.

Fireworks go off.
I will hide under the bed.
I'm not scared – really!

Interludes by
Nelson LaPurr, Edmund, Nitro, and Xing Lu Pierce, with a little help from Cheryl Pierce.

MIDNIGHT MEOW

Midnight Meow is an ink-black kitty—
Shines like patent leather, ever so pretty.
He sparkles in sunlight and lies at his ease
In a window sill, regally, sniffing the breeze.

He quickly jumps up and runs to the door
For his dinner that waits in a dish on the floor.
Later, he curls up all in a heap
On Dad's chair in the corner for another short sleep.

Midnight's a porch panther, but in his dreams
He stalks the wild tapir and hears monkey screams!

UNCLE EEKER

Uncle Eeker was a gentleman cat
In a grey velvet tailcoat (but no top hat).

His whiskers were many, majestically lush,
And his snug, tidy boots were snow-white plush.

His silky shirt-front had never a wrinkle;
His big yellow eyes—oh, how they twinkled!
He sauntered and strolled, never pranced or gamboled,
While cats of less dignity from his path scrambled.

Refined in his manners, pristinely attired—
The most elegant kitty of all ever sired—
From exquisite nose to faintly-ringed tail,
His demeanor was purrfect to the last detail.

From humble beginnings, he rose to the station
Of King of the Cats, Top Cat of Cat Nation,
The Tsar of All Felines, whose law was his whim
(Or so he believed; and we never dissuaded him!)

REQUIEM FOR A BEDSPREAD

Some cats like cloth and some like wood,
Other work in plaster.
Whatever medium they choose,
Their craft they quickly master.

To rip, to shred, to gouge, to slice
Is what they all desire;
A surface that would yield to claws
Was all that mine required.

"A scratching post's for wimps," he said
With silent feline laughter.
"Texture's what I want to feel—
That's what I go after!"

A bedspread, newly monogrammed,
Offered tactile pleasure
Of the sort that my sweet cat
Cherished as a treasure.

Silky thread and satin fabric
Flew in gay profusion
Until his paws were satisfied—
Then he settled down to snoozin'!

XING'S SECRET WEAPON
(originally posted as, "Beware of flying objects", by Nelson LaPurr)

well, this morning, mom hadda go change her pants before going to work. she peed 'em. before breakfast. and it was all xingxing's fault.

xing likes to sit on the table that the puter face sits on while mom types. all of a sudden, xing started that well-known rhythmic urping that signals an imminent hairball (and she, being very fastidious, hurls them frequently). mom didn't wanna annoy xing just then by moving her, so she just moved papers outta the way and told her to go for it; which she did.

but the hairball didn't come all the way out! it hung about half-way out the pipe, so xing panicked and did a scrambling, floundering about-face turn to jump up on the puter body where it sits next to the face. while she did this, her head went through a 180-arc with her mouth pointing upward, spraying hurl-juice ceiling-ward with great success.

then her head followed through with a snap, disengaging a world-class hairwad, which smacked into the wall—four feet away!! it slid slowly down the wall like those icky garden slugs, and plunked onto the carpet. us boys watched in awe. we've projectile-yakked a few times, but NEVER anything like that. xing has a new weapon, and we respect her for that. we're staying outta the way when *she* hurls.

oh, yeah; it took mom almost three minutes to get herself together enough to go clean up the mess, wipe her eyes, and use her asthma inhaler. and then, of course, to change her britches.

How To Train your Human Slave
HRH Yao-Lin

As an egotistical and demanding Siamese Prince, I consider myself an expert on all matters relating to training your human slave. My methods have been tried and tested by myself with real success, and I feel I should impart this knowledge to my fellow cat friends, especially the younger readers. Should you choose to commence this training program, I will be available for advice and reassurance on a daily basis. Don't give up - it will be worth it in the end.

How to train your human slave

1. Make them believe that you love them. Use affection, purrs, big sad eyes, plodding etc. This is the first and most crucial step in ensnaring your slave- use it wisely and never to excess. If you master this, the rest of the training will become simple.

2. Do something the human's think is clever and/or cute. Good examples include: choosing a toy

and dropping it at their feet, climbing the curtains, watching and chasing objects on the television, playing with your siblings. Choose your moment wisely – all of these actions need to be completed at a time when the humans will notice i.e. when they are sat in the living room.

3. Make the slaves feel guilty. If they haven't refreshed your water, begin to drink from the washing up bowl or, better still, lick the bath suds. If your food bowl is empty, begin to chew on your sibling or on your toys. Do not stop until they have provided ample refreshment.

4. Never assume that the slaves understand you. Speak S-L-O-W-L-Y and L-O-U-D-L-Y to get your point across. The louder the YOWWWL the better, although occasionally a small yet shrill howl can be just as effective. Once again, choose your moment to convey your request – one of the best times is when the humans are sleeping. Approach them slowly and then HOWWWWL in their face. A guaranteed reaction. Repeat as necessary until they fulfil your demand.

5. If you are unhappy with the menu at your current accommodation, simply refuse to eat for a few days. This will send your slaves into a flurry of panic and, whilst you can anticipate at least one trip to the vet, you will eventually find the cuisine you are served is healthier, tastier and most importantly, far more expensive than usual. Do not settle for sec-

ond best: fresh meat from the butchers and premium quality biscuits are what any royal cat deserves.

6. Be hospitable to any small people visiting your premises. They are what the slaves refer to as 'children' and if you pretend to like them, the humans will gush about how friendly and adorable a pet you are. Of course, you can give little ones the odd nip when nobody is looking, but be careful. Small humans are unpredictable and can be hostile when provoked (trust me, I know).

7. If your human approaches you for affection, ignore them. Better still, walk away or jump up to a surface area they cannot reach. If they manage to pick you up, struggle until they are forced to place you down again. This will keep your slave on his toes and will ensure that they react with unexpected delight and pleasure should you eventually approach them for cuddles.

8. If fresh meat from the butchers isn't quite quenching your palate, steal food from the human's plates. They usually have set meal times. Ensure you are present for each meal and proceed as directed. They will give in if you persist.

9. If your human is not cooking your dinner quickly enough, launch yourself, with all claws and all paws, at their back. I usually begin by howling and, if I am still being ignored, I jump and then climb up their backs as though they were a tree. I will climb

up as far as I can before the human eventually manages to shake me off. Apparently this causes the human pain. Do not sympathise – it is an effective technique to make your dinner arrive more quickly. Other humans present will find this amusing and it will also serve as a 'cute and clever' thing to do, thus reinforcing the training process.

10. If you wish your litter tray to be cleaned more regularly, walk around in it and then leave poo prints all over the house. Make sure you walk all over and inside the bath, any sinks, all clean surfaces and especially any clothes scattered around.

11. If your human is annoying you, use your claws. Grab any exposed limb (I prefer arms) and wrap yourself around it. Kick with your hind legs and, if you get the chance, sink your teeth in. After two minutes, stop. Look at the human with 'big eyes'. Begin purring and rubbing your chin against any wounds you may have inflicted. The human will become confused and believe that you have merely been playing. When they then move in for a cuddle, start the whole process again. NB: - can provide hours of amusement, especially on highly-strung individuals.

12. Demand a space in your human's bed. They usually have electric blankets and thick duvets so under the covers really is superior to your cat bed. Follow the humans and then climb under the quilt. Refuse to budge. If they manage to force you out,

wait until they are asleep and then scratch their noses and bite their hair. Humans require up to 8 hours of solid sleep a night. This procedure takes only days to work as it is in your power to ensure your slave gets only 5 hours of broken sleep. After no more than a week, you will be able to claim your rightful spot under the quilt whenever you wish.

13. Remember: Persistence is the key. Your slaves will soon realise that resistance is futile and will worship your every move without hesitation.

Should you choose to commence this training program, I will be available for advice and assistance at all times. Good luck!

MOM
Merlin Schumacher

1

I lived in this house with stairs for awhile in Poiland. It had carpet I shredded and lots of places to hide. Next door, it had a dog in a yard who sounded pretty interesting. I had a yard too, but could I go outside? No, I was banned from exploring my own yard because of "stinging centipedes the size of snakes" according to Mom. I wanted to go into the dog's yard. I really did. I figured his yard was probably safer.

One night, Mom left the big sliding windows open, so while she was talking on the box at her ear, I opened the door. A talent I've had since I was really little, I'm proud to say. I was nice enough to let my sister Shadow out with me too.

Shadow wasn't as adventurous as I was. She stayed in the yard. I didn't. Who wanted to meet stinging centipedes when there was an interesting dog next door?

So off I went.

About this time I heard Mom say something about "the door being open and oh no what was up and here was Shadow but where was Merlin and oh my god he was a housecat and didn't know how to take care of himself outside and why didn't anyone tell her the screen door latch was broken and hopefully he didn't go near the rottwieler next door." I didn't really listen; I was on a mission.

Let me tell you that this desire of mine might not have been the healthiest I've ever had. Come to find out, the dog next door was NOT friendly. No, he wasn't, and he was big. Actually, that might be an understatement. He was huge, and he not only didn't like me visiting his yard, he was going to remove me from his yard…..in tiny little kitty pieces.

I swear that's what he yelled at me, as he charged all barking and slobbery jawed, his eyes popping madly out of his head and his breath steaming in the air.

Yep, every little hair I had stood up on end, and before I could say "eek" my legs took off. Thank goodness the rest of me is connected or I might have been in little pieces before that dog even reached me. As it was, I think I tinkled a little on my way under the fence. I might've even left a more solid present for that dog, not that he deserved it.

I've never run so fast or hard in all my life. I was a blur. Nothing was left of me in that yard but little furs floating in the air and a broken fence board. I was gone, and that was the problem. I ran so far; I got lost. I didn't know where I was.

2

Mom searched for me late into the night, calling my name and looking all over. Dad finally convinced her to go inside by telling her I would probably be back in the morning waiting at the door to be let in. You can plainly see who I matter more too. Like I could even tell where the door was. I had to find the house first.

I finally fell asleep exhausted from running and then being scared and lost. The next day, no door, no house, no food, no Mom, nothing. I was still lost and hungry.

Mom searched again in the morning and by afternoon she had made a paper with my picture and her name and number on it. She posted that paper everywhere she could think of, by nighttime, she was crying and worrying that I would never come home. So was I.

The next day Mom searched more. Then she called the humane society where I came from and asked if I had been turned in or caught. Come to find out, I have some kind of chips inside of me with numbers on them that the professionals can read. But no me, not anywhere. She called the people who clean up the road kill and shelters, everywhere. Then she sat up all night on the porch waiting for me to come home. I didn't. I wanted to, but I couldn't find her.

I was so scared and so sad without my Mom. I was confused, but I told myself I was not going to give up looking, not now, not ever 'cause I knew my Mom wouldn't.

3

Not to long after Mom hung the papers with my handsome pictures on it, she got a call from a man who lived several streets over. He had adopted a little stray cat that lived out on his porch. Lately, a really large black cat had been coming around and picking fights with his little stray. He thought maybe it was me.

Mom was so excited that she went over immediately and started looking for me in the area, calling my name and searching all over. Her heart was breaking, but she didn't see any cats around but the little adopted stray.

Boy was Mom disappointed, but she asked the man if he would call if he saw the big black cat again, anytime day or night. The man promised he would.

That very night the man called. "The big cat is here again."

Mom grabbed her cell phone and started out, but to her disappointment, the big cat was gone. The man, however, was there.....with all his guests.....having a dinner party on the porch.

Mom thanked him for calling, said hi to everyone, and searched the area again, but no big, black cat. The man saw her disappointment and offered to let her sit in his yard and wait for the cat to return.

And do you know what? Mom did. She sat there waiting, with her phone in her hand and all those people looking at her like she had lost her mind.

But the best part was I had found my way home. So while Mom was sitting in this man's yard, her phone rang. It was Dad telling her I had just shown up and walked in the door and was eating.

I'm not sure what Mom said, but when she came home we both lay down in her bed, me with my head on her shoulder, and we slept straight through until morning. We were exhausted from my adventure.

The next morning Mom said she hoped I had learned my lesson, and I have. I now know it is better to face cat eating snakelike centipedes than rabid foaming dogs any day.

The Ideal Gift For Your Human
HRH Yao-Lin

Last night my human slave neglected to clean the litter tray at the appointed time.

This task is usually completed by 9pm thus enabling me to frequent my toilet at various intervals throughout the night, safe in the knowledge that it is both clean and fresh smelling.

Due to a lack of training on my part, or more likely, utter stupidity on her part, the female slave 'forgot' to clean the litter tray last night.

This morning, she was awoken by the delicate waft of poo. Stumbling out of bed, she wandered, bleary eyed, towards the bathroom where she found, and almost stepped in, two large steaming presents, left for her by none other than His Royal Highness.

"Oh, Your Highness," she said, still bleary eyed, "thank you for these most magnificent presents. I bow to your superiority, my Royal Master". To which I responded with an evil glare.

Ok, that doesn't sound altogether feasible. What she actually said, in between wretches, was " Oh For

F*** sake I have to clean up cat s*** before I have even had a coffee - and it's my day off!". To which I responded with an evil guffaw: Mwa ha ha!

Well, I think the human has well and truly learned her lesson. Next time she neglects to clean the litter tray, I will leave her *several* steaming parcels instead of just two. Serves her right for being lazy.

An Introduction To Baby Mao
Baby Mao

Hello! My name is Baby Mao. I am a tabby point Siamese Cat and I live on the Isle of Wight with my big brother Yao-Lin. I also smell of poo. I can't help it. I just do.

I used to feel bad about being smelly but then I realised something very important:

Just because you smell of poo, it won't stop people loving you.

Really, it's true! I have a Mummy and Daddy who love me very much and no matter how smelly I am, they never ever shout at me. Also, I have an adorable girlcat who lives on the other side of the world. Her name is Kaia and she too is a tabby (or lynx) point Siamese! She doesn't mind that I smell of poo, or that I leave a trail of poo prints wherever I go. She says that even if she lived within smelling distance of me, she would love me just the same. I love Kaia, I love my Mummy and I love my Daddy too. I even love my big brother Yao-Lin although he is mean sometimes.

So you see, if you are a smelly cat then don't feel bad –you too can live as full and rich a life as I do!

Love and hugs
Baby Mao

Casper

Dean McCaughan
(better known as Jasper McKitten-Cat's Dad)

I have a pet cat. I know this to be true even though, honestly, I haven't seen it for several years. But the evidence is there — I refill food bowls and empty litter boxes. Occasionally I awake and there is an unexplained warmth behind the crook of my knees. But there is no visible proof. My wife gave it a cute name, Snowball. I thought Phantom was more fitting. She got angry with me over that, telling me that was a mean name for such a nice cat. So we compromised and she lets me call it Casper after the Friendly Ghost.

Once, I was sick and had to stay home from work. I fell asleep on the couch and dreamt of something heavy yet soft on my chest, humming and vibrating the illness out of my lungs. When I awoke I was warm and I could feel my head starting to clear, the congestion loosening in my chest.

I still cannot say I've seen our cat in many years (and sometimes I still question his existence) but in the rare mornings when I wake and the covers are warm against me a feeling of calm comes over me and I can't help but smile knowing he's watching out for us.

Sometimes:
a tale of human stupidity
Tilli

There's one thing I don't understand. Humans have their uses, yes.. opening packets, supplying 'nip and toys, creating laps and lovely strokes… but why, WHY do they have to be so stupid?

Take my Human, Jessa. She feeds me, strokes me, supplies toys and all the normal human things. And then.. she goes and takes my toys and gives them to another kitty. And why? Because I don't play with them.

Rubbish. Just because I don't exactly play with them all the time.. or at all… that's no reason to give them away!

Oh, I guess I better introduce myself.

My name is Tilli, and I'm a cat. I'm mega-cute, with yellow eyes and a pink nose. I'm black and white, and so pretty. You should worship my prettyness. You should worship me anyway, of course, but more so because of my prettyness. Yeah. Worship me!

Ahem, anyway.

So, she's gone and given my toys away, and that's not all. Why does she insist on hugging me all the time?? I'll be suffocated one day soon! I am not a teddy bear to be hugged constantly, despite my sweetness. I swear, I might pull a Psychokitty on her and poop on her pillow. If Max doesn't mind of course. So anyway, sometimes, I worry about that human's sanity.

Wait, what am I saying? Sanity? Humans have no sanity.

So anyway, that's all I wanted to tell you. Go buy me some treats or 'nip. Or new toys! Off you go, go on.

An Introduction to the Siamese Cat
HRH Yao-Lin

Greetings my inferior subjects. Allow me to introduce myself.

I am a Royal Siamese Prince who is waited on paw and foot by my adoring human slaves. I live on the Isle of Wight, which is adequate, if a little quiet for my delectable tastes.

I enjoy eating, sleeping, eating, sleeping and being fussed over (when I am in the mood). If you wish to befriend me, there are a few simple rules, which, if you follow, will allow us to gain somewhat of a rapport

Rules

1. Do not approach me. I will approach you if I am interested. Otherwise I will simply ignore you.

2. Do not disturb me when I am eating. This is my most pleasurable of pursuits and I will

not tolerate being bothered whilst I am engaged in this.

3. Do not assume that I am cuddly just because I have a huge tummy. I gained my girth through months of eating and it is neither a measure of my cuddliness nor a sign of cuteness. I am a Royal Prince.

4. Do not disturb my human slave whilst she is cooking my dinner. Food is priority over conversation.

5. Do not fuss over my little (inferior) brother whilst in my presence. To do so will only result in a jealous display of aggression on my part. You have been warned.

6. If I lay on your lap with my belly exposed, I wish for it to be rubbed. I will bite you when I have had enough.

7. Follow each of the above rules. To do otherwise will displease me greatly and, as any human slave to a Siamese will know, a displeased Siamese is *not* something to trifle with.

Remember, now you are in the company of a Siamese cat, you may consider yourself truly blessed.

Ta ta for now
HRH Yao-Lin

Song of Torment of Stinky Brothers
Shadow Schumacher

I sit up high just out of reach
Watching you walk by underneath.
As you think you're the only one
Sneaking 'round and having fun,
I'm getting ready to pounce and land
Upon your head biting your hand.

Running lightly on his feet
Big boy then crouches on his seat
Wiggling his butt back and forth
Waiting to jump on Ko Ko dork
Off to the right I watch for a chance
To jump and wreck his crouching dance

Only when they least expect me
Only when they cannot see
That is when I take my vengence
On my brothers slow and dense

We Are Still The Kitties...

Sniffing, walking nose to the ground
You follow a bug wandering 'round
Deep in hunting concentration
And predatory situation
I wait my chance to scare you silly
Scattering you thoughts willy nilly

You think you'll catch me as I rush
Keeping quiet in nighttime's hush,
But little do you comprehend
What makes my world lightly spin.
It's my lifetime's work tormenting
My brothers, and making them scream.

Yes that is what makes my world turn
And I don't think you'll ever learn,
So I will continue wrecking havoc
While you both complain that I pick.

Wrestling each other on the ground
Tossing, biting, spinning around
Scratching, rolling, bunny kicks
Then stopping and giving little licks
Growling with your ears laid back flat
I jump and land right on the pack.

Lining up getting ready to run
Racing is another big fun.
You both act like little kittens
Running, looking for lost mittens.
Smiling enjoyment of the race
I smack that smile right off your face.

So maybe now you will see
Why it makes life so fun for me
To torment both those stupid boys
My brothers, my living toys.

~Shadow

My Life With Kitty Cats
E.J. Smith

A four-year-old awaiting her very first, very own kitty-cat is one of the happiest, and most impatient, people in the world. It was a late winter Saturday in February of 1986 when I eagerly sat on my parents' bed, kicking my feet while Mom finished getting ready. My sixteen-year-old sister sat beside me and asked what I might name my new pet. With as much conviction as a preschooler can muster, I replied "Snow White." There was no doubt in my mind. The beloved Disney version of a fairy tale classic was my favorite character, so it made sense to me at that time to name my first pet after Snow White. I had told my parents I wanted an all white cat. They did the good parent thing and told me that it was possible the kitty-cat place wouldn't have any all white kitties. Somehow, I knew I would be coming home with a white kitty-cat that afternoon.

My parents, sister and I left for the shelter and a little while later, though it seemed like an eternity to my four-year-old self, we arrived at the local Humane Society. I just about went kitty-cat crazy in that pet shelter. Kitties, kitties, kitties everywhere! Every place I looked, there was a kitty-cat, meowing for attention. I wanted them all! It wasn't very long into my frenzy when I spotted the most beautiful kitty-cat I had ever seen: a blue and gold odd-eyed white short-hair, about a year old, standing quietly and patiently in her cage. She looked at me and I looked at her and it was most definitely love at first sight. Her tail perked up and she meowed sweetly at me. My parents and sister finally caught up with me from the other room as I knelt down to stick my fingers through the bars of the cage. She let me rub her head and began to purr. It didn't take long for my parents to realize she was "the one." Mom let out a chuckle and commented, "The name tag on this one's cage says 'Sugar.' Seems appropriate." I looked at her and said very matter-of-factly, "Her name will be Snow White."

Mom and Dad took care of all the paperwork and my sister carried Snow White out to the car. We placed my new kitty-cat in the cardboard box we brought with some towels and blankets in the bottom, since those were the days before pet carriers. I chattered nonstop about how happy she would be and how I would play with her and make sure she had plenty of food and water and just on and on about everything we would do together.

Over the following years, Snow White and I spent many happy days and nights with each other. She was very patient, constantly begging for food, knowing she would eventually sucker someone into giving her a little of whatever they had, if for no other reason than to get her to leave them alone. She knew the precise moment the can of wet food was opened every day. The family was never sure if it was because of super sonic hearing or if it was her sense of smell. Snow White always knew when there was meat around. I made a joke once about her olfactory skills and said, "The Nose knows." She would come into the kitchen, nose high in the air, sniffing as hard and as fast as it could. Snow White also was the type of cat who would let you pick her up and "love on her," as Mom would say. I would scoop her up, rub my face on hers and kiss the top of her head. I often toted Snow White around like a baby doll in the early years of our relationship. She rarely complained and never purposefully bit or scratched me. She was the perfect pet for a kid who "just wanted to play with the kitty-cat."

As I got older, I would still play with Snow White and talk to her. She became more of a "lap cat" and I was usually more than willing to accommodate her. It was a rare occasion when I told her I didn't have time for at least a little attention. She kept me company when I was sick and comforted me in her own special ways when I was sad. Friends and boys came and went but Snow White was always there to listen. She even helped me with my homework once. I had to write a children's book for Spanish class; she was one of the co-stars of *La Gata y el Pez* (*The Cat and the Fish*). Instead of drawing pictures, she very patiently posed for me while I took photographs.

During the time our family had Snow White, we acquired two more cats, both female strays; one from a golf course and the other found by a friend of my sister. Trudy was a black cat with white splotches and Cheshire was mostly light brown with a dark brown tail and a raccoon mask on her face. We took them in and loved them all equally, but Snow White was my first kitty-cat and always held an extra special place in my heart and I in hers.

High school started for me and I wasn't home as often; I kept busy with band, choir, the school play, academic clubs, dances, athletic games, church activities, etc. I no longer had as much time either of us would have liked for my feline friend. Around the same time, a hospital stay of my only living grandparent prompted my parents to build a home big enough to house them, Grandma, my sister, the cats and myself. The family knew it would be hard on the pets and everyone else, but we all made the move without too many problems and the kitty-cats had a new place to explore.

The time came in early 2000 when Snow White began to get sick. She didn't have any particular feline disease except old age. Our family estimated she was around fifteen years old then. Over a period of two months, she didn't eat very much but would constantly drink water. She slept a lot and, when she was awake, would roam slowly around the house, meowing frequently and like she was in pain. We took her to the veterinarian and were told she had lost a lot of weight and her kidneys were failing. The vet gave us a few options which we took some time to think about at home, but we all knew it was time to let her go.

My parents, sister and I took Snow White back to the vet the following Saturday, March 4, 2000. It was an unseasonably cold beginning of March. Once again, we prepared a box with towels and blankets to take her home after visiting the vet one last time. In her younger days, she was the type of cat who would scare easily once you got her in a vehicle. She would want to roam around the car, look out the window and meow loudly to make sure you knew she was displeased. That day, Snow White calmly let me hold her in my lap as I spoke softly to her and told her I loved her and would miss her more than she would ever know. Somehow, in those short few minutes of the drive to the vet, I think she understood.

We all filed into the building, Mom and Dad holding hands, my sister holding the box and me, holding Snow White. Mom and Dad checked in at the desk and we were ushered in to one of the examination rooms. The vet came in soon after. He said he would give Snow White a shot, she would pretty much fall asleep and eventually stop breathing, and it would all be without pain. He left to get what he needed and to give us a chance to say goodbye as a family without him there. We all petted her and told her what a good kitty-cat she had been and that we loved her. She mewed a few times as if to say she loved us too. The vet came back and we left the room so we didn't have to see him give her the injection. A few moments later, he let us back in the room and we were with her until the end. I scooped her up one last time, held her close to my chest, kissed her on top of her head and said, "I love you." She looked me in the eye with her two beautiful mismatched ones and closed them. I felt the life leave her now-limp little body and I knew, unfortunately, this was no fairy tale where I could wake my Snow White with a kiss.

We placed Snow White in the box we had lined with blankets and covered her up. The box was then closed up and we left the clinic. I carried her in her box out to the car. As we walked across the parking lot, it began to snow, ever so softly. It was then that I knew my beloved kitty-cat was at the Rainbow Bridge, being welcomed by God and all the other pets and animals that were adored by their owners. My eighteen-year-old self cried frequently over the following week. My favorite furry friend of the past fourteen years was gone from my arms and lap, but not from my heart and memory. Snow White has since been laid underneath a small stone angel statue in my parents' garden. I know she waits for me and my family at the Rainbow Bridge, along with Trudy and Cheshire, who have also since passed. After all three kitty-cats were gone, Mom put her foot down and said, "No more. I can't handle getting that close to another pet this soon." I could understand her feelings, but I was ready for another pet; a house without pets just isn't a home.

A couple years later, even after Mom's edict, my family has collected five more cats: Smokey, Schwartz, Casper, Sassy and Tigger. Four of them are shelter rescues, courtesy of the local large chain pet store, and one was acquired from a pet store in a trade agreement. The time of year was February once again, this time in 2003, and Mom mentioned one Sunday afternoon that she and Dad were taking Grandma to the local large chain pet store to look for a cat to adopt. Grandma was often home by herself and, though she had a canary, my parents felt she might be happier with another pet to keep her company. Mom asked if my boyfriend and I would like to tag along and we agreed to go.

I love looking at animals in pet stores. Walking into the pet store that day made me feel like I was four years old again, looking for a kitty-cat to bring home, but this time I didn't get my hopes up that Mom would say I could bring one home as well. She made it clear we were only looking for a cat for Grandma. It was a Pet Adoption Weekend so there were lots and lots of animals waiting for new owners. I walked around, looking at all the pretty kitties, this time much more subdued than the last, seventeen years previously. Most of the kitties needing a home were fully grown and rescued from different parts of the area. Grandma found a few that she liked and took her time to decide.

This time it was Mom who found me and showed me a beautiful, all-white kitty-cat with golden eyes. He was sitting quietly in his cage when he looked at me directly in the eyes and let out a little "mew." My hand went up to my mouth as I gasped at the sight before me. A store employee was close by and I asked if she would open the door so I could pet the pretty kitty. She unlatched the door and as I held out my hands to pick him up, he jumped into my arms. From that point, neither of us said a word. I stroked him and he nuzzled my face. I had to close my eyes to hold back the tears I could feel coming. I didn't even have to say anything before I heard Mom tell the store employee, "It looks like we'll be taking this one home, as well."

In total, our family took four cats to their forever home that day. I adopted Casper, Grandma rescued Sassy and Mom and Dad took in Smokey and Schwartz. Sassy was a stray, found by workers at the steel mill a few towns over. She was very skittish at first but has learned to love all in the house. Smokey and Schwartz were left as a pair at the Humane Society with no note or any indication of who they had belonged to or their health conditions. Even though Mom was the one to say "no more pets," she told me later that if I took Casper with me when I moved out, she and Dad would then be without a cat all over again. Mom then decided they needed a cat as well. She liked Smokey and Schwartz both and just couldn't bear the thought of breaking them up, so they got to come home with us that day.

Tigger came to live with us a few months later. Sassy had a penchant for knocking over the bird cage, so Grandma decided to give the canary and all of its equipment and extra birdseed to a locally owned pet shop. While she was there, the shop owner's kittens were roaming around the store and one of them hopped up on the counter. He was small and scrawny and very cute. Grandma asked the shopkeeper, "How much for the kitten?" He told her that since she had just given him her canary and a bunch of bird supplies, she could take the kitten at no charge.

All of the kitty-cats have unique personalities and have their own roles in the household. Smokey has green eyes and sports an all-gray fur coat except for a very small white spot on his chest that Mom calls his necklace. He is definitely the king of the house and kitties and rules his roost. Smokey likes to think he has control over his people as well and we all know he does. Schwartz wears his bright yellow eyes with a completely jet-black pelt. He is higher in the pecking order than the other cats but desperately wants to be king. Instead of calling him the prince, he has been dubbed the Duke to honor Dad's favorite actor, John Wayne. Schwartz mainly keeps to himself but has been known to grace Mom's lap with his dark fur. Sassy shows off her brown classic tabby and white Maine Coon fur with greenish-yellow eyes. As the only girl, she is definitely a spoiled little princess. She struts around and knows she is hot stuff. Sassy is the smallest of all the kitties but has no problems holding her own amongst the boys. Casper has golden eyes and looks crisp and clean in his all-white fur. His job is the court jester, constantly doing crazy kitty things to make us all laugh. Casper reminds me of like Snow White in many ways, like his sweet demeanor, but different enough that he has his own personality. Tigger looks like the cartoon cat Garfield with his red classic tabby and white Maine Coon markings, golden eyes and rotund body. He is low man on the totem pole but doesn't seem to mind. Carrying on with the royalty theme, anyone can see by his girth that Tigger takes his job as the royal food taster very seriously. He doesn't really care if Smokey likes their food or not; Tigger just loves to eat it.

I spent several years with all of the new feline friends before moving out on my own. Friendships were made and cherished, bonds formed and nurtured. Life has changed quite dramatically since those first days of my relationships with Smokey, Schwartz, Casper, Sassy and Tigger. Not only did I move out of my parents' home, I moved to a city halfway across the country. I married my high-school sweetheart and now live with him. I was sad to leave my kitty companions when I left for my new home in a big city far away, but I was fortunate enough to take at least one of them with me. Casper shares the apartment with my husband and I. He does all of his crazy kitty things in a much smaller space now and can get very annoying, especially during the night. Casper's favorite trick is to hop up on the dresser in the bedroom, hop to the top of the television on the dresser, hop to the top of the set of shelves next to the dresser and then into the middle fabric bin on the top shelf and curl up in it to sleep. If that isn't enough, getting down is even more fun. Casper jumps from the top shelf to the television, steps on a lower shelf of the unit and then leaps onto the bed where my husband and I are sleeping, usually pouncing on my legs or stomach. All of this is done around three in the morning. Even with all of that and the other goofy things he does, I wouldn't trade him for anything in the world.

Kitty-cats have always played a big part in my life. They have been playmates, companions and comforters. Some days, it seems like Casper misses his purring pals back at my parents' home. It must be lonely going from four other cats with you at all times to being by yourself most of the day. I've often thought about making a feline addition to our new household. Who knows? My husband, Casper and I might have a new kitty-cat story of our own in our future.

Ode to Cod

Cod is great and
Cod is good
Cod is soft and smells so good
Cod is cooking! says my nose
Cod always makes me streeetch my toes

I'm glad my Mom cooks Cod for me
I do my Cod dance gleefully
Who'd guess that such a simple fish
Prepared by Mom becomes a DISH

If a bit is left for me to eat
The next day it is still a treat
Mom nukes it till it's warm and tasty
Hot would *hurt* and cold is hasty

Oh Cod, sweet Cod,
I love you so
I'm very sad you'll never know

- Edsel The Pooch -

You Know You Are a Cat Blogger When....
By Baby Mao's Mummy & other cats! *

You know you are a cat blogger when:

1. Food isn't referred to as food in your house. It's all stinky goodness.

2. You no longer refer to people as people. They are either: humans/slaves/Not the mama/Lap lady/Tasty face etc etc

3. The people you regard as your closest friends live on the other side of the world. Oh, and they happen to be cats.

4. You know what a Meme is and feel thrilled every time you are tagged for one. Of course, the humans you talk to in your day-to-day life just don't understand.

5. You really REALLY want to teleport over to

Daisy's house and play dress up with her.

6. You understand this acronym: WWJD**? and know it doesn't relate to Christianity!

7. You feel really really excited that your cats have blogging girlfriends/boyfriends and you have already started thinking of themes for their weddings.

8. You are so happy to have found other humans who are as cat crazy as you!

9. You feel strongly about 'nip addiction and see it as a serious threat to society.

10. You get withdrawal symptoms if you don't log onto the cat blogosphere site at least once a day.

11. Your cat gets more emails than you do.

12. You have thousands of photos of your cats stored on your computer. You would be hard pushed to find one of you or your family.

13. Your first thought of the day is ' oh, it's Meezer Monday/ Tabby Tuesday/Wordless Wednesday etc' today!

14. If anything happens to you, you are going to leave your pets to the blogosphere. You just KNOW they will have the best lifestyle a cat could have!!

15. You want to join the Tuxedo Gang hideout cos it sounds so cool.

16. When you see something pink, you think of Skeezix.

17. You've started looking at everything in terms of "I need material for the blog. How can I use this?"

18. Your human family members comment about what they read on your cat's blog.

19. You go on an eight-hour road trip to see friends, but all 200+ pictures you download from your camera are of 'vishus deer' related sightings.

20. You go to bed WAY past your bedtime because you were getting the next day's blog post ready.

21. You take a camera with you to the vets office.

22. Your blog posts become dinner discussion

23. Your gurlcat is halfway around the world.

* Other cats include One Eyed Jack, Daisy, Kaze, Latte & Chase, The Crew, Millie and The Meezer Gang.

** What *would* Jeter do?

Calendar Cats
Karen Jo Gray

January cats are tired of the snow.
They wish it would just pack up and go.
>   Their greatest desire,
>   As they dream by the fire,
Is for backyards and meadows free from the snow.

February cats know Spring is on the way.
This thought cheers even the gloomiest day.
>   When it's dreary and dark
>   They glow with the spark
Of the promise of buds on the trees down the way.

March cats hide inside from the howling wind.
They know that strong gusts are not their friend.
>   A kitty-cat kite
>   That sails out of sight
Is a fate all of them hope to forfend.

April cats are nobody's fool.
They don't pay taxes or go to school.
>   They have it made
>   As they sit in the shade
Of a tree where the breezes are cool.

In May a young cat's fancy turns to . . . BUGS
Wherever they hide, even under the rugs.
>   Look, there on the screen!
>   That one's being mean,
'Cause he's on the outside. Oh, those vishus bugs!

June cats love the flowers so fair.
Open the window and they'll sniff the air
>   Full of flowery smells.
>   They'll twitch their tails
And inhale deeply of the good fresh air.

July is a month that most cats agree
Is full of loud bangs that makes them flee.
>   Fireworks are pretty
>   In country or city,
But the booming hurts kitty ears, don't you see?

August kitties get left home a lot
While their families seek a vacation spot.
>   They can throw a party
>   And celebrate hearty,
Teleporting over to the kitty hot-spot.

September kittens love to chase leaves,
But something in the older cats grieves
>   Just a bit for warm naps
>   In sunspots and laps
With the fierce summer sun hanging over the eaves.

October cats have fierce glowing eyes.
They creep through the dark, their beans to surprise.
>   But it's all in fun;
>   A mile they would run
If a real spook showed up with red-glowing eyes.

November cats are ready to feast.
They've been smelling turkey since the sun rose in the east.
>   They purr thanks and bow
>   Their heads in a vow
To be really good kitties, right after the feast.

December cats are full of cheer.
They know that Santa will soon be here.
>   They climb the tree
>   With obvious glee
And purray for Peace on Earth througout the year.

Aliens Amongs Us
Dee Francis

SETI, (the Search for ExtraTerrestrial life and Intelligences), researchers listen to the heavens for the radio signals of intelligent beings on another planet. This search has been ongoing since the mid-1960's. To date, they have not found been successful in detecting the presence of another civilization. Even if they should find a signal, would they be able to understand it and its meaning?

On our own planet Earth, there is currently a great diversity of life. Some of these lifeforms even live with us in our homes as our pets: mostly kitties and doggies. Any pet owner will tell you that their pet seems to have a mind and personality of its own—that the owner doesn't understand (but obviously very different compared to humanity's). Unfortunately, a great many species, plant and animal, are being driven out of existence by Man in his lust for greed, raw materials, and living space.

All of the higher animals are aware of their environments. Almost all scientists agree on this fact. Many of these animals show signs of emotions and some even crude reasoning (by Human standards).

(Animals have such a different way of thinking!) Some scientists dismiss these facts as a bias upon the part of the observer(s). (Can't make the animal seem too Human; equal in status to us. Though what does makes a Human a Human?)

Almost all animals make sounds that are understood among their own kind. I wonder if this means that the sounds our kitties and doggies, (or any of the other animals), make are really some kind language that we, Mankind, don't understand. Of course, even amongst Humans who speak the same language, does the other person really understand what the speaker is truly saying?

I do know that when my kitties rubs against my leg, headbutts me, or purrs while being petted, it brings me joy. I hope that I make them happy by giving them my attention and affection. I feed and take care of them. To me, they are my children. I do NOT need to comprehend the way they 'think' to love them. I just do.

"A Meezer's Thoughts About Life and the Pursuit of Food During Banishment Because He Agreed to Participate in a Loser Leaves Town Match with His Brother and is Now Living in a Tent in the Wilderness in the Living Room with his Girlfriend, Sanjee"

Miles Meezer

(Thanks to the gang at Forty Paws for the title)

- ::whaps forehead:: don't lay on your back and bunny kick during the match! That's how you get pinned!!
- How long can I lay here with my head sticking out before mommy says "aww, is you camping you cutie?"
- Tent tipping is fun. Except when you want to get back in and the entrance is pointed towards the floor.
- Don't lay on your back when you're rassling!!! ::whap::
- What time is she going to bed? I need to go scavenge for foods.
- Is ham a wild food?
- What about roast beast? It's beast, so it must be.
- Oooo, nip toys. I didn't know there were nip toys in the wilderness.
- Who keeps leaving their stinky shoes in the wilderness? Sheesh, the smell is wafting into my tent.
- I need a grill.
- Where's my fishing gear?
- ::sigh::
- How long will it take for Mommy to start hollering back at me if I start hollering?
- 3.2 seconds – she's improving.
- Yep, I definitely demand a re-match – Loser has to shave their furs off.

A Tribute To Mao's Testicles
Baby Mao

You followed me
I followed you
We were like each other's shadows for a while...
Now as you see
This game is through
So although it hurts
I'll try to smile
As I say...

Goodbye, so soon
And isn't this a crime?
We know by now that time knows how to fly
So here's goodbye, so soon
You'll find your separate way
With time so short
I'll say so long
And go...
So soon...
Goodbye!

Mooch-Feline Hobo, Beloved Friend
Shawna Howes

Back during the depression, hobos used to leave symbols in areas where other hobos could see them. These symbols let them know whether or not a place was safe, if there were cops that would hassle them, or if food or work could be gotten there, all kinds of things. The symbol for "kind hearted woman", someone who would give them much needed help, was a stick figure of a smiling cat. I think our homes have always had this hobo sign drawn on it by the local cats, because we've definitely seen our share of hobos. Mooch, however, was in a class by himself, as you will soon see.

My fiancé, Chris, and I have always had a soft spot for kitties. We both grew up with cats in our homes, and we've continued the family tradition. We've always had at least one cat, and usually we have two or more. While one was adopted from a rescue organization, the others have all been strays that showed up one day, sometimes crying and sick, others just asking for food, and were overjoyed to find a loving home for the rest of their lives.

There were some that came by, gladly ate food and went on their way. Some became a neighborhood fixture, coming every couple of days for food, water, and attention. We couldn't take them all in, of course, but we did what we could. Sadly, some of those vanished without a trace. We would feel horrible when that happened, because we couldn't save them all. We knew, though, that any difference we could make would be much appreciated.

One day last summer, I sent an email to an ex-boyfriend of mine I hadn't seen in years, wanting to know how things were going. At the end of the email, I told him to pet his Bombay cat, Zeeep, for me. I'd lived with him and Zeeep for about two years, and, after we broke up, I took care of Zeeep for several months until he could get a job that would let him be home more often to give him attention.

I was shocked to get a short reply from him. Zeeep had died two years ago, from complications of diabetes. He and his friends had gone on vacation and boarded him at a vet's, and he died there while they were gone. I was heartbroken. He had never told me about Zeeep's death, even though he knew how to contact me.

During the next few days, I felt terrible. If only I had stayed in contact with my ex-boyfriend, maybe I could have taken care of Zeeep while they were gone, and maybe he wouldn't have died.

At around the same time, we started having a regular visitor. A large, stocky tomcat, jet black fur and golden eyes, started coming onto our porch and sleeping there. He didn't do anything else, just would go up the steps, throw himself full-length, and take a nap. We started going out when he was there, and, unlike most strays, he didn't run away from us. In fact, he was very affectionate, purring and climbing into our laps, obviously happy to get head skritches and tummy rubs. We started leaving food and water out for him, and he started to announce his presence by a loud meow when he showed up.

We told ourselves we weren't going to keep him, we were just feeding him. Never mind that's what we thought with most of our other cats, we were in happy denial. Oddly enough, our two cats, Kahlan, a lovely tortoiseshell girl, and Ashe, a white girl (she had a grey smudge on her forehead as a kitten, so she looked like she went through an Ash Wednesday service…it vanished when she grew up, so everyone wonders why we named a white cat named Ashe), who are very territorial about who comes around even though they're indoor cats, didn't seem to mind him at all. Instead of exploding into hisses and pounding the window to get him to leave, like they did with any other cat that came by, they just watched him. He seemed to like the feline attention too, and would talk to them through the window.

Soon, he was walking towards the front door when we'd turn around and go back in. "Sorry. We can't let you in." we said, and he always looked disappointed, but accepted what time we could give him during the day when he showed up.

I thought at first that he was someone's outdoor cat, because he was so healthy and well-fed. I found out from both of my next door neighbors that they were also feeding him. We started joking that he would come over, ask for food, to use the bathroom, bus fare... Even though one of our neighbors was calling him Midnight, we started to call him Mooch, because of his regular string of suckers, and that name stuck. We also discovered that his home base was under our house. We'd heard cats meowing under there, sometimes so well that our cats got spooked by it.

Around September, we learned how strange Mooch was. One day, as I was turning to go inside, he meowed at me. I stopped, looked at him, and said, "OK, jerk, come in." and he followed. He engaged in some mutual nose-and-butt-sniffing with the girls, went over to the food bowl, emptied it, drank some water, came into the living room and took a nap on the couch.

Thinking he didn't know where to go potty, we picked him up and showed him the litter box. I have never seen a cat look both horrified and disgusted at the same time. His look seemed to say, "You mean they all go to the bathroom in the SAME PLACE?"

We figured that he'd be like all the other strays we'd let in the house, who always stayed. However, after his nap, he went over to the door and meowed to be let out again. We'd never seen this before. A few of the cats we'd taken in tried to get out on the first day or so, but once they realized this was for real, they calmed down. Mooch was clearly asking to go back outside. Surprised, we let him out. We thought he'd be back and would stay the next time. That didn't happen. He clearly liked us a lot, but he didn't want to stay as a permanent roommate.

The days usually went like this. Usually he'd show up around afternoon or evening. He'd meow loudly to let us know we were there. Sometimes he would claw gently at the living room window near where we sat to get our attention. He'd come in, trot straight to the food and water, usually emptying both. Sometimes he'd go from there right back to the front door and ask to be let out. We'd tell him, "Hey, this isn't a dine-and-dash, you know." Other times, he'd saunter around the house, get on our laps, talk to us in a way that sounded like he was telling us how hard his life was, and take a nap on the couch or upstairs on the bed. After his beauty rest, he'd eat some more and then leave. Gradually, he started visiting more than once a day.

What was stranger was what he didn't do. I kept a close eye on him the first couple of visits. I knew he was an intact tomcat, so I expected him to spray or poop in a corner, marking his territory. He never once, in the entire time we knew him, went to the bathroom in the house. I know he wasn't using the litter box, which continued to repel him, but he wasn't going anywhere else, either. I'd had a few cats that'd been strays that had a little trouble at first with the idea of the litter box, and there were a few accidents. Not with Mooch. If he needed to go, he asked to go outside, and he'd be gone for a few hours, probably taking care of errands, we said.

He didn't fight with the girls, either. Kahlan, who's definitely the alpha cat here, and has defended that title against many claimants to the throne, didn't seem to even care he was there or not. Ashe, who, at the time, was still about half-grown, kept hissing at him and trying to start a fight. Mooch, who was almost twice her size, seemed bemused, but he didn't take any crap from her. One time she charged him, and he shoved her away so hard she sort of slid a yard back. She'd try and bat at him, and he'd deliver a strong smack. There were a couple of verbal arguments, ones that made me glad I couldn't understand exactly what they were saying, but there were no knock down, drag out fights.

As October came around, I started getting a little worried. Sometimes bad things happen to cats on Halloween, especially to black cats. We had some rowdy teens in the neighborhood, and I was starting to have nightmares about what they might do to a friendly black cat cruising the streets. Chris and I decided that Mooch would have to stay the night on Halloween. But how would he take that?

I talk with my cats all the time. Just because they can't speak English doesn't mean they can't understand what we're saying, at least a little bit. I told him that in a few days, he'd have to stay the night in order to be safe from bad people who might want to hurt him. I didn't know how much was getting through, but I just wanted to prepare him. When Halloween came around, he showed up around 5 in the evening. He walked over to the door about two hours later and meowed.

"No, Mooch. Remember what I said? This night isn't safe for you to be outside, so you can stay with us." Amazingly, he understood. He didn't ask to go back outside again, curled up on the couch, and went to sleep.

When I woke up the next day, he was gone. Chris came over to me when I came downstairs.

"It was the weirdest thing. About 6 in the morning, he walked over to the couch, stood up, and pawed at me gently until I woke up. When he saw I was awake, he started talking, and I swear he was apologizing for waking me up so early, and then he went over to the door, stood up, batted at the knob, and turned to me and meowed. He was apologizing for not being able to open the door on his own!"

Mooch didn't have a pattern to his visits, or his overnight stays. Sometimes he stayed the night, other times he didn't. He'd stay most of the day, and the next he just came over for some food and left right afterwards. Sometimes external things made him change his mind. When I had the flu, he stayed the night the whole week, curled up with me and sleeping with me the whole time. This was nice, but a little frustrating, as he was so big. He'd wrap his paws around my leg when he slept, which of course meant I couldn't turn over! He complained when I moved, but settled down and went back to sleep.

We live in Oklahoma, and our weather can be pretty bad. One night, we had a terrible thunderstorm and a lot of rain. Mooch hadn't come in that day, and we were really worried.

Suddenly, we started hearing very loud, scared

sounded meowing right under our feet in the dining room! We immediately recognized it was Mooch. Chris threw on his shoes and a raincoat, grabbed a towel, and ran outside. He went over to the small opening on the side of the house that led underneath. We knew that was his front door, we'd seen him go in and out of there often enough. Chris called to him, and he crawled out, let himself be wrapped in the towel and carried inside. We dried him off and warmed him up. He stayed the night that time.

Then we got a major winter storm, and, again, we heard him crying. Chris started putting on his cold-weather gear. This took awhile, so I started talking to Mooch through the floor, which would have looked strange to anyone who'd see it.

"Mooch, run over to the front door as fast as you can. You'll get a little wet, but we'll dry you off and get you some food and warm you up, OK?" I said this over and over while Chris suited up. He unlocked the front door and started to open it, and was nearly bowled over when Mooch shot through the door as soon as he had room and ran to the food bowl. We looked at each other in amazement. He knew what I was saying and did it. He purred as I rubbed him down with a towel, not missing a bite.

There was another storm that produced an even more poignant moment. Chris had suited up to get him from under the house, but, even after calling his name several times, he didn't see Mooch. Then he crawled over to the opening, reached out and patted Chris's hand, but wouldn't come out any farther. He was telling Chris that he was OK, and he didn't need help. I'd never seen a cat act so solicitously before.

Our friends got used to us suddenly standing up in the middle of a conversation in order to open the door for Mooch. Sometimes he sat on their laps. Other times, like on Friday nights, when we have people over to play Dungeons and Dragons, he'd eat, watch the goings on, get on the battle mat and paw at figures and dice, then leave.

For a few months, I was going to a daily program for the mentally ill (I have bipolar disorder, also known as manic-depression). I was picked up and dropped off by a van provided for people who didn't have transportation. Mooch started waiting on the porch for me to leave, pet him, and let him inside when I left. Sometimes he walked me to the van, as if to make sure I got on safely! Several times, the driver and other people in the van chuckled when we pulled up to my house at the end of the day. Mooch was usually lying on the porch waiting for me, and he'd trot over to the van, talking the entire way as I got out and said goodbye, then he'd walk me to the door and go in with me, most of the time.

I found out that one other neighbor let him inside, but he never did what he did with us, staying for hours and sometimes spending the night. In that home, he'd come in, go to the food bowl, eat, play with their small dog, then turn right around and ask to be let out. He didn't spray or poop inappropriately there, either. We were the only people who he'd hang out with and crash from time to time.

By this time, we were pretty resigned to the fact that he wouldn't stay with us as an inside cat. We started saving up money, though. If we couldn't make him stay outside, we'd get him neutered so he wouldn't contribute to the large stray population we have here in this neighborhood. Maybe he'd stay after that, maybe he wouldn't, but it was the least we could do.

As a tomcat, Mooch got into the requisite fights with other cats. Interestingly, he particularly started running off other tomcats that showed up and tried to hassle Kahlan and Ashe through the windows. He usually won these exchanges, but not without some scratches, scraps and bites, though they all seemed minor.

That all changed one night when he came inside. After he had himself some dinner, he sat next to me on the couch, and I started petting him. He'd had a nasty scab on his head he liked me to scratch around, and I started doing so. Without warning, the scab burst, and a lot of thick yellow-white pus started pouring out of an abscess I didn't know was there. I hollered for Chris to get me some Kleenex to clean him up, but the pus just kept coming and coming. It must have hurt, because he started trying to get away from me, and started running around the house, pus still leaking from his head.

We were very scared. It was late at night, and we had no vehicle, let alone money for a trip to the emergency vet hospital. We didn't know what to do, and now he wanted to go outside, fighting us when we tried to mop up the pus. We were afraid if we didn't try to clean it out, he'd get blood poisoning, and would probably kill him quickly

Finally, I lost patience with him. "OK,. If you don't want help, fine. But I'm not letting you outside like that. You can stay here, and, if you want me to make it stop hurting and make it feel better, I'll be upstairs," and I turned on my heel and walked away and went to the bedroom to read.

Ten minutes later, he slowly walked in. He looked at me, deliberately came over to the bed, hopped up, walked over to me, went into "cat-loaf" mode, as we call it when he's on his folded legs, and just looked at me. I went downstairs, got some warm water, dishrags, cotton balls, and hydrogen peroxide, and came back.

I proceeded to start cleaning the wound. He grunted a few times, but otherwise didn't make a sound or try to move away. I used hot compresses to get the pus out, and he started to purr a little, pressing his head into the warm, wet cloth. The hardest part was when I had to probe and squeeze the wound to get the gelatinous, semi-solid pus core out. I know it had to hurt, because I'm sure I felt the pain almost as bad just having to do it, but he didn't fight me. I flushed the nearly quarter inch deep crater it left behind in his head with water, then hydrogen peroxide. I knew a bandage was right out, so I left it alone after that.

Then I put him on my lap and gave him a good petting, while I called my mom and asked her for help, as she's had cats all her life, and has helped out strays. She told me I'd done basically all I could at that time. There was no money for a vet follow up, but prayers are free. I started calling all my friends and asked them to pray for Mooch's recovery. I blessed him with holy water and let him sleep with me that night.

Thanks be to God and the many prayers, his wound healed clean and filled in, leaving only a small scar easily covered by the hair that grew back. He was soon back to his old self again.

As the seasons turned, I started working outside in the backyard, preparing a vegetable garden. Many times while I was out there, Mooch would sit a few yards away and watch me digging and moving dirt around. Sometimes he came over and inspected my work, looking at me like he seriously doubted my sanity.

One of the best memories I have of him was probably in March. I had woken up early to find there was a definite chill in the air, but it was clear and sunny. I poured myself a cup of coffee and saw Mooch was sitting on the deck out back. He meowed when he saw me in the window looking at him, so I put on a warm barn coat, and went out back to sit with him.

It was maybe eight or so in the morning. It was a little chilly, but not too bad. My breath steamed along with my coffee. I lit a cigarette and Mooch and I greeted the day together. He sat next to me, leaning into my petting, purring so loud I was surprised Chris couldn't hear it inside the house, sometimes mowing happily when I talked to him. It was just one of those perfect moments that you want to last forever.

April came around and the weather started getting warmer. Correspondingly, Mooch stayed inside a little less than he did during winter. One day, he didn't show up at all, and that night we were worried when we still saw no sign of him.

The next afternoon, we came back from the grocery store, and he was curled up by our garbage bin. We greeted him, and he lifted his head up, looking wearily at us, making no move to get up and come inside. Something inside told me to tell Chris to pick him up and bring him in. He purred when he got picked up, but otherwise didn't move.

We put him on a pillow on the couch, and he looked like he appreciated it, but didn't move around much. We thought maybe he had a cold and felt lousy. I was petting him, when I stopped and looked closely at his skin under the black fur. Instead of the normal pink-white, it was lemon yellow. I looked at his eyes, and instead of gold, they were the yellow of a highlighter. I yelled for Chris to get a hold of someone to take us to the vet, because Mooch was badly jaundiced.

My godson's father, Dan, came over in a hurry. He liked Mooch, who liked to sit on his lap to get pettings. Angela, my godson's sister and good friend, came with him to give me some emotional support. Mooch didn't fight me at all when we put him in the carrier and we got in the truck.

The walk-in vet clinic we chose was luckily not full. They showed us into a room quickly. The vet winced when he saw how yellow he was, especially when he peed a little on the table, and it was bright yellow. He took him in the back to get blood work done. We waited for a long time.

When the vet came back, he was very somber. "I've never seen a living cat with a bilirubin count so high. He should be dead. He might have gotten into something that caused liver damage. I don't know if we can save him, but he needs, at the very least, a massive blood transfusion and IVs, because he's badly dehydrated. What do you want to do?"

I knew Mooch was a fighter. I knew also we didn't have a lot of money to spare, but I couldn't just let economics be the sole deciding factor. I talked to Dan, Angela, and called Chris, and we decided to give him a chance. At least we might find out what was wrong and get it treated. The vet explained about payment plans we could use, and started giving me forms to sign to authorize treatment.

"Oh, and I need you to sign this authorization for feline leukemia and FIV testing, if he's never been tested and he's an outdoor cat. That's the first thing we need to do: eliminate those right off the bat," he said, as I got to the end of the stack of papers. I just signed it like I'd signed all the others. Then he told us to go back to the waiting room while he ran the additional tests.

Five minutes later, he came out, holding something in his hand, and I didn't like the look on his face as he motioned us back into the exam room. He placed in front of me a little plastic thing that looked an awful lot like a pregnancy test but with two windows. And there was a big bold, unmistakable plus sign in one of the windows. This was the combined FeLV/FIV test.

"He has feline leukemia. He's probably had it a long time, and he may have been born with it. There is nothing we can do at this late stage. I'm sorry."

Through my tears, I called Chris and let him know the bad news. I asked the vet, "There's no way he can recover from this?"

"No. The other tests show that his liver and kidneys have failed."

"Is he suffering?"

"Yes. It's not going to get better, and it's only going to get worse. He's not hurting now, but the strain on his body will soon be too much, and he will be in pain until his heart gives out."

It was the hardest thing I've ever had to do in my life. The vet let me in the back of the clinic. Mooch was reclining in a cage, and I got him out. I walked around, carrying him, telling him I loved him, and I was sorry I couldn't make him feel better. I told him he was going to the Rainbow Bridge to wait for me, and that he'd be able to play with all the other pets there. He'd have a home, and he'd never have to leave again, and when I got there, I'd take him to heaven for me.

While the vet updated records, he asked me a little about Mooch. "You do know you probably extended his life by several months by caring for him, don't you? He probably wouldn't have made it through the winter without all the food, shelter and love you gave him," he said, and I felt a little better. We had made a difference in his life, even though we couldn't save him this time.

I mentioned the abscess he had had, and the vet

was amazed it healed up. Most of the time, he said, the FeLV virus impairs healing. A wound that infected should have ended up killing him, with it being on his head and all.

I let Dan and Angela hold and pet him, and I kept petting him while the vet and a vet tech got the shot ready. Mooch showed a flash of his moxie when he growled at the tech when she shaved his leg so they could have a better view of his vein. He yowled and hissed at the vet when the needle went in, being his old feisty self again for a few seconds before he passed away.

We brought him home, and the next day we buried him in the backyard, at the spot that he would sit at and watch me in the garden. Now he could continue to watch me always. My neighbor gave us a piece of marble for a headstone. We plan to have it engraved someday, with the stick figure of a smiling cat and the words:

MOOCH
200?-2007
Feline Hobo-Beloved Friend.

It's A Four Letter Word, And It Starts With "M..."
Max the Psychokitty

I'm getting used to it, and that's sad.

My People have implemented the M-word 4 times in the last 4 years. The longest I've stayed in any one place is 2 years; cripes, I'm 6 years old and have lived in 8 different places, if you count where I was born and then the place where the Younger Human got me (I wasn't there very long; just long enough to wrack up a big emergency stabby place bill from getting caught inside a reclining chair, which convinced those Very Young People that perhaps they could not afford to keep me in the style to which I should become accustomed.) No kitty should have to do that. People should bring the kitty home, and then stay there until the kitty is ready to run off to The Next Big Thing.

(Don't be sad. We all know The Next Big Thing involves rainbows and a bridge, but it's not a scary place for us. Besides, I'm pretty sure the Stinky Goodness there is on-demand, PLUS it's made out of Twinkies, and I for one am looking forward to Twinkies whenever I want them.)

But, like I said, I'm getting used to the M-word. And I'd be lying if I didn't admit that I like investigating new places; there's a weird little thrill a kitty can get by exploring new houses with its new smells and nooks and crannies. What I don't like is when the M-word begins with a car ride, because car rides never end well. They either end up at the stabby place, where the bald guy sticks things where things simply don't belong, or they end up being four-day-long sessions of Torture The Kitty, whereupon I say over and over "Take me home," and the People either say "Please stop whining," (which I am NOT doing) or "I'm sorry…it's only 500 more hours until we get there."

This time, when the People were forced into the M-word by a landlord that first said "Oh, I'm not going to sell my house" and then said just 5 or 6 weeks later, "Oh, by the way, I am selling my house so you have to get out," they managed to do the whole thing without sticking the kitties into a car. The house next door was available, so they decided to spare the kitties the horror of even a five minute ride in the car, and rented it.

For once, they thought of the kitties.

It started out all right; for a week or so before M-Day-1, the people were busy putting things into boxes, and I knew what it meant and was really ticked off because I didn't know we weren't going to be forced into the car for days on end; Buddah Pest, on the other hand, was clueless and thought they were making all these boxes for him. It was like a veritable kitty jungle gym, and he jumped from box to box, oblivious in his joy.

I fumed, though I did not poop on anyone's pillow in my anger. I was good and waited to see just how bad it was going to be. I mean, I survived it all those other times. How bad could it be?

Then one day they scooped us up and marched us to the house next door, where we were free to explore its vast emptiness.

This was way cool; I could smell other kitties but I knew they weren't there anymore. I could even smell a dog, but I was sure he was long gone (surely the People would not let us loose in an empty house where a DOG was hiding...they might not be bright but they're not entirely stupid, nor are they intentionally cruel. I don't think, anyway.) I went from room to room, sniffing and snooping, peeking into closets, going up and down the soft, carpeted stairs.

Buddah slinked upstairs, found a closet in which he could hide, and wouldn't budge.

Weenie.

He just doesn't understand the sheer joy of exploration; I suppose all he could fathom was that he was jerked out of his own little world and thrust into someone else's, a world with no boxes upon which to jump, no Supreme Commander Kitty Tower, and no toys.

Buddah without toys is a sad little kitty.

In one room of the empty house I discovered the People had brought over a bed and a climbing tower, as well as food and a litter box...and there was my blue plastic tomb, since they brought me over in the blue plastic tomb, fearing that once my fur was exposed fresh air I would erupt into Rambo Kitty, drawing blood and fighting for my own personal freedom.

Remember the blue plastic tomb. It's important.

After a while, when they were satisfied I had explored as much of the house as I could, they picked me up, rescued Buddah from the closet, and locked us in the room where they had placed our stuff. The Woman said she was sorry, but we had to be there, and then told us to just stay there and everything would be all right.

There was enough in the room to be comfortable for a whole day, even though it was with each other and that doesn't always work out so well...but I wasn't done exploring. I know there was a bathroom I hadn't scoped out. I'd been in the kitchen but I hadn't pulled any of the cabinet doors open, and sometimes there's crunchy treats hiding behind cabinet doors.

I did what any inquisitive kitty would do: I stuck my paw under the door, curled it upwards, and pulled.

Lo and behold, thusly did the door open.

I could explore!

And I decided to be a good and thoughtful kitty; I knew the People would be in and out, carrying heavy objects and boxes, so I decided to stay out of their way. They worked hard for a good 45 minutes, and had brought something particularly heavy in through the front door when I just had to speak up.

I mean, I had discovered the coolest of closets—one that was under the stairs and went ALL the way under; it even had a little nook in the back. I was sure they didn't know about it so I said, "Hey! Look at this! It's wicked awesome!"

The Woman laughed and said she could hear me through the air vent, I must be upset about being locked up.

With a heavy sigh, because they are limited by their puny people brains, I stepped out of the closet and said "No...look at this!"

But they didn't look; no, instead of checking out the awesomeness of the closet, they began freaking out. They slammed the front door shut; they ran to the room where the rumbly bikes would sleep and slammed that door shut. And then they began running around like they had eaten that stuff they're always telling me that if I eat it, flames will shoot out my ass.

The Man called out, "Buddah!"

The Woman called out, "Buddah?"

And they went from room to room, looking for that little black furball.

The first place they went was the room in which we had been locked; he wasn't on the climbing tower, he wasn't in the blue plastic tomb, and he wasn't in the closet, cowering behind the litter box, which is good because that would have been gross.

Giant human feet pounded on the floor as one of them checked every nook and cranny upstairs and the other one ran around downstairs, both of them calling out Buddah's name. I climbed halfway up the stairs, trying to not roll my eyes at them, and sighed heavily, "Hey."

No one looked at me.

"He got outside." The Woman was frantic. "He got outside."

They threw open the front door, darting out in a panic, slamming it behind them.

"Hey," I said again, to no one in particular. I waited a few minutes, and then went upstairs to look out the window; they were walking up and down the street, calling "Buddah! Booooodaaa!" over and over, and I felt bad because they were all very upset.

I heard the door open again and the Woman was back, hoping that somehow she had overlooked her errant kitty. I jumped down and ran back to the landing on the stairs and said "Hey," but again she did not listen. She looked and looked, and then ran back outside.

Her eyes were all red, and she had snot running down her face. Snot. Running. DownHerFace.

I went back to the window; the Younger Human was getting into his car so he could look for Buddah in a wider range. The Man was talking to neighbors, and I was sure he was asking "Have you seen a little black kitty? He's very young and he's never been outside without a leash, and it's very, very hot today..."

And then, after much time had passed, after the Woman put Lost Kitty fliers on the community mailboxes, after the Woman had come back into the house several times Just In Case, and I said "Hey" to her over and over, they gave up.

They could not find Buddah, but things still had to be moved.

I jumped down from the window and went to wait on the stairs for a bit. They left the doors closed, only opening them when they had something to bring inside. The Woman hauled in boxes, and I said "Hey" to her and she said I was a good kitty, but she did not listen.

She moved a big chair in, jamming it through the door, and she was still crying, so I said "Hey," one more time, but I knew by then she was not going to hear me. Her head was stuffed with being sad, and she couldn't hear anything more than "Buddah is gone, I will never see him again" pounding around in her head.

In all that sadness, they decided I should be back where things were familiar, because I obviously wasn't moving from my spot on the stairs. The Woman picked me up and took me outside, and while she was walking from one house to the other I know she was looking for a wandering black furball.

So I was back home, which looked like its insides had exploded in a mass of Holy Crap, It's M-Word Day #1, and she put me in the Younger Human's office, which still had my tall climbing tower.

So I went to look out the window and watch them implement the M-word; I'd never seen it in action before since I was always locked in a bathroom when it happened. It was fairly boring, and I almost stopped watching when I saw the Woman sit down on the grass under the tree in the front yard. She kept looking up and down the street, and I know she was hoping to see a sliver of little black kitty peeking out from behind a bush or even someone's car.

And she watched cars go by; they seemed to be going a lot faster than normal, even I could see that, and I knew she was afraid Buddah would not know how to react to them.

I knew she was thinking that Buddah, who is not afraid of the vacuum cleaner, is wary of people he does not know so he wouldn't go to anyone who called to him, but he loves the outdoors and would be happy to explore it even when he's afraid to explore a great big empty house.

She sat there and cried.

The Man kept moving things, because it had to be done, and he had the choice of worrying in one place or worrying while he worked. He kept moving.

All the sudden I heard the man, whom I could not see because he had taken various amounts of crap to the new house, yell out *I found him!* and the Woman jumped up from her seated position of woe...I have never seen a fat woman move so fast. She was past where I could see before I could suck in a deep "If you'd just listened to me" breath.

The Man was holding Buddah, he later told me, hugging him so tight he thought he was going to pop, and the Woman ran up the stairs, crying even more as the Man handed Buddah to her.

"You're never going to guess where he was," the Man said.

I don't think the Woman cared, she was holding Buddah just as tight as the Man had.

"I came upstairs and heard a meow...he climbed out from under Max's tomb."

Yep, they had searched the house high and low, had looked in that room four or five times, looked in the blue plastic tomb, but little weenie kitty, in all his little weenie glory, had wiggled through the tiny slot at the bottom of the tomb and curled up under there.

He was *under* the blue plastic tomb.

There was much rejoicing, and they squeezed him again and said "You're going home."

The took him back to the old house, where it looked like every room in the house had thrown up, and let us loose for a while, so they could catch their collective breaths and have some lunch, and where they called the Younger Human, who was in his car headed for That Damned Job to let him know that the biggest pain in my backside was safe.

We got treats. They can't find Buddah, and we got treats.

That's People logic. I'm not arguing about it because I enjoy my crunchy treats, but we were rewarded for their ineptitude.

Okay, perhaps that how it should be.

Later on, they picked us both up and put us in an empty bedroom with a bed I sometimes liked to use, and with food and water. The Woman said she was sorry again, but they still had to work, but we would be able to stay there the rest of the day, and wouldn't have to go to the new house until everyone was ready to sleep there, and then we would all go together and stay there together like a bunch of happy little pansies...

All right, I'm paraphrasing what she said, but cripes, it was getting to be like a freaking love fest.

When the door closed—and I knew that door wasn't going to open now matter how hard I pulled on it—Buddah asked "What's the big deal?"

"They thought they lost you," I said.

"I wasn't lost. I knew right where I was."

"I knew right where you were, too, but would they listen to me? No. I sat there on the stairs and kept trying to get their attention so I could show them where you were, but they got themselves so riled up that they couldn't hear me."

"The Mom said to stay there," Buddah said, "so I stayed there. I woulda gotten in trouble if I didn't stay there. Did you get in trouble? You didn't stay there!"

"No, because I stayed in the house," I reasoned. "I knew better than to go outside."

Buddah was quiet for a very long time. We napped, we ate, and napped some more when he asked in his tiny little kitty voice, "Max, do we have to go back there?"

"We're going to live there," I told him. "It'll be all right. All our stuff will be there, and the People will be there, too. Nothing bad is going to happen."

"I'm scared," he admitted.

"You were so scared when we moved here that

you hid inside a big chair and wouldn't come out," I reminded him. "That turned out okay. The People aren't going to take you someplace that's not safe."

"Promise?"

"I promise," I said. "And for just a little while, I'll be nice to you so you don't have to be afraid."

And he wasn't.

When the People finally took us to the new house to live, Buddah took a deep breath and explored; he found his toys and his climbing tower and the place where the kitty treats would be kept, and decided it would be all right. He could live there forever.

I haven't told him we're going to do it again someday, because we always do. And because I heard the People say that the next time, we're going to move into a House That We Own, maybe in two years. I'll leave Buddah in ignorance for now, so he doesn't spend two years worrying.

No, I'm not being nice.

I just don't want to hear him whine for two years.

Yep, that's the reason.

How Can I Be Losted When I Know Right Where I Is?
Buddah Pest

I don't know what the big deal was. The Mom said "stay here" so I stayed there. I didn't like it because the room she put Max and me in smelled like other kitties, and I'm pretty sure they were like the Rude Outside Kitties that Max says we're supposed to hiss at and bang on the windows at so they run away, but I've never actually been furry face to furry face with a Rude Outside Kitty and I don't really want to be because they're RUDE.

That's not a nice thing to say, I know, but they really are rude. They walk around our back yard like they own it and they POOP in the grass and everyone knows that you poop in the litter box and you bury it even though I usually forget that last part of it which gets everyone upset because they gag on the smell, and I know the Rude Outside Kitties don't always HAVE litter boxes, but they could at least go next door where there are flower beds with dirt and they could go there and bury it. I know they could because I used to live next door and I looked outside a lot and it seemed to be a fine place for a kitty in need to poop.

But we don't live there anymore and that's why Max and I were put in a room that smelled like Rude Outside Kitties AND a woofy. We loved the house next door because it had wood floors that were fun to slide on and stairs that made it sound like we weighed fifty-teen pounds when we ran on them, and there were high places we could get to and make the Mom and the Dad say things like, "Well aren't you a clever boy!" and "Please don't fall" even though we're cats and we don't fall, except for that one time Max jumped wrong and really did fall, even though he says it was on purpose to prove he could fly. It was a perfect kitty house, but the guy that owned it said YOU HAVE TO LEAVE and the Mom and the Dad said lots of really bad words and got all mad, but in the end they started getting boxes and put all their stuff into the boxes, which was fun because I got to play with all those boxes, I jumped on them and played inside them and no one got mad when I chewed on the corner of one of the box flaps and no one got mad when I scratched at one of them because it smelled a lot like my special scratching toy.

I was having 124 kinds of fun with the boxes and wanted to keep them all but Max said the boxes were not a good thing, it meant the M-word was imminent and we needed to be Really Really Mad but I couldn't be Really Really Mad when I had so many boxes to play with. He said "Just wait, you'll see" and then one morning came and the Mom and the Dad picked us up and took us outside. OUTSDE! Where the Rude Outside Kitties are. I didn't see any Rude Outside Kitties, but we weren't outside very long. The Mom and the Dad went into the house next door and set us down and said to look around, because this was our new home.

But I didn't want a new home, and I didn't like how it smelled. I wanted to find someplace to hide because if I could hide then it wasn't really happening. But Max, who kept saying the M-word was the worst four letter word a kitty could say, was all happy and said "Whoa, this is wicked cool" and he started looking around to see what there was to see and didn't seem to mind at all that it smelled like Rude Outside Kitties AND a woofy. He just wandered around, looking, and when he started up the stairs I followed him because I was pretty sure Max could keep me safe, especially it the woofy was still around.

When we got upstairs there was a closet and I ran inside and went to the very back of it and curled up tight so that it wasn't really happening, but Max kept wandering around with the Mom and the Dad and I stayed in the closet until 162 hours later when the Mom came in and said "Ok Big Guy, we have to lock you up now" and she picked me up and put me in a bedroom with Max. There was one of our climbing towers and a bed and Max's blue plastic tomb, and in the closet there was a litter box which meant I couldn't really hide there, and there was also some food and water, but not in the closet with the litter box because that would be gross.

That's when the Mom said "stay here," and she closed the door. Max wasn't happy because he wasn't done exploring and said there was lots of stuff he hadn't seen yet and he wanted to see it all, and that's the fun part of the M-word, seeing all the nooks and crannies in a new house, but I wasn't having any fun, not at all. I just wanted a place to hide.

After a little while Max said "well, screw it" and he stuck his paw under the door and pulled, and it came open! Then he said "let's go look around a little more" and I said "No, we have to stay here and I want someplace to hide but there's no place to hide and I want to go home!" And that's when I realized there was a place under Max's blue plastic tomb where I could curl up and hide so that it wasn't happening. I had to really wiggle hard to get under it, but I got in there and curled up and then nothing was happening.

Max went out and explored, and a few times the Mom and the Dad came in and "Buddah? Buddah?" but I was hiding so nothing was happening, and when nothing is happening you don't have to answer.

Later I heard Max say "Hey" but no one said anything back to him. He said "Hey" a lot but no one said anything back any of the times so I figured he was finding new fun things and saying "Hey" because he thought they were spiffy or something. In between saying Hey he called out to me and said "Come out! You're making the Woman cry!" but I didn't hear anyone crying, all I heard was Max saying "Hey" and the Mom and the Dad saying my name.

After 200 hours went by Max said that if I didn't come out the next time someone called my name he was going to come up the stairs and stick his butt in the opening under the blue plastic tomb, and pee on me, and I believed him because he's been looking for an excuse to pee on me for a long, long time.

But then 62 hours went by and I didn't hear Max; I heard the Mom and the Dad mumble about taking him home, and then nothing.

So when the Dad came in I didn't wait for him to call my name, I just wiggled out and said "Hi!" and he got really excited and picked me up and shouted out the window "I FOUND HIM!" but that was kind of silly because I wasn't lost, I knew right where I was. The Mom was outside sitting on the grass and she jumped up and ran into the house and up the stairs and the Dad let her hold me too and she really was crying.

And then they took me home! I was back in the house where everything smelled like it was supposed to and Max was there and we got some crunchy treats! I was very happy but he said to not get too used to it because sooner or later we were going back to the other house and we would live there, but it would be all right, and I didn't need to be scared.

Well sometimes Max says some things that aren't true because he wants to get me into trouble so I wasn't sure about that, but when I asked him to promise he said he promised, and he was really nice to me for 3.64 seconds and said he would be nice to me for just a little while when they took us to the new house for good. And the next day the Mom and the Dad picked us up again and took us to the house next door where it still smelled like Rude Outside Kitties and a woofy, but it had most of out stuff in it and that smelled like Max and Buddah. I promised Max I wouldn't hide, so I crept around and checked things out, and I wasn't scared anymore.

I think Max is right, the M-word is the worst 4 letter word there is. I don't like it, not at all.

Max even told me that I wasn't smelling Rude Outside Kitties, it was nice kitties who lived in the house with their pet woofy, but they weren't there anymore and I didn't need to worry about them. I was safe from them, and I could relax.

That's when he pushed me down the stairs.

The 31
Max the Psychokitty

1. If someone other than the primary food giver opens a can of Stinky Goodness, it should not count as a meal; it is a snack, and the primary food giver should then feed the kitties more later in the day.

2. If there are two kitties in the house, and the People call one of the kitties "Sweetcheeks" once in a while, then they should not be surprised if the other kitty takes it upon himself to determine if those cheeks really are sweet. And if they are not, they should not get upset when the kitty who did the tasting whacks the other kitty over the head with his paw, because the supposedly sweet kitty really only tasted like cat spit, and that is very disappointing.

3. If you sleep with some fancy schmancy thing covering your eyes to block out the light, the kitty has the right to wedge his paw under it, lift, and then let it snap back to your face in order to wake you up in the morning. Kitties are hungry even when you want to sleep in.

4. It is always funny to have sixteen pounds of cat dropped onto a person's face in the morning; there's no point in getting upset about it. Part of a person's job is amusing that cat, and the cat thinks it's really funny.

5. If you are not sitting at the table and you have food, it is acceptable for the kitty to stick his face into your edible business; if you don't want kitty help, eat at the table where he understands the rules are no sticking your face into what the people are eating.

6. If you go hunting and bring home 50 cans of Stinky Goodness, it is not fair to stack them up in the cupboard and not give the kitty one of them. If the kitty sees you putting the cans away, it is your duty to make him happy and open one for him. If the other kitty doesn't hear, it sucks to be him, but open a can for the observant and watchful kitty.

7. If a kitty makes the effort to throw up someplace where it's easy for a person to clean it up, the person then owes the kitty at least 5 crunchy treats. If the person fails to reward the kitty with crunchy treats, the next time he throws up it will be in your shoe.

8. If one kitty is running down the hall, screaming, and the other kitty is running behind him with his mouth attached to the first kitty's butt, the biting kitty should suffer some kind of time-out, or

maybe even get their furry little hide duct taped to the nearest solid object.

9. There must be fresh live dead shrimp on a kitty's birthday. And kitty crack. Without those two things, it's not a Happy Birthday. A person can make the birthday even happier by adding some steak in there somewhere.

10. If you do not want a kitty napping in your basket of freshly laundered clothes, then put the clothes away before the kitty discovers them. Once a kitty sees the basket of fresh clothes all warm from the dryer, it is his right to curl up on them.

11. If a kitty hacks up the Hairball Of All Hairballs, it's not nice to ask "is your tummy empty now?" Of course it is! Clean up the mess, then open a can of Stinky Goodness!

12. Clean kitchen counters feel good on a kitty's tushy, so don't get all bent out of shape when, within 2 minutes of scrubbing them sterile-clean, the kitty jumps up there and rubs his butt cheeks all over them. Look, we do it when you're not looking anyway, so what's the point of getting upset?

13. On nice days, the People should not go out and do things, they should stay home and keep the windows open for the kitties, so we can enjoy the nice breeze, too. Really. It's not fair to be out riding around on rumbly bikes or whatever when there are kitties at home waiting for fresh air.

14. If the kitty growls at you for whatever reason (it's probably because you annoyed him) don't stick a finger in his face and wiggle it and say "We don't growl." Because obviously, one of us does, as evidenced by how upset you are.

15. If you don't want one kitty to push the other kitty down the stairs, then tell the other kitty to not sit so close to temptation.

16. The first rule of making muffins: the kitty always gets a bite.
The second rule of making muffins: the kitty gets another bite.
The third rule of making muffins: If the kitty doesn't get a bite, something is going to meet an ugly, ugly toothy death.

17. If a person leaves anything out upon a kitchen counter that can be rolled, spun, or batted around, it belongs to the kitty by default. This included potatoes, bottle tops, and eggs, although eggs can typically only be played with for 2.41 seconds.

18. Eggs left on the counter top should be hard boiled to extend the kitty's span of amusement.

19. Things left on the bathroom counter also belong to the kitty by default. Your ~~drugs~~ medications are fair game, especially if the pills rattle in the bottle nicely.

20. Never presume your toothbrush has not been tested by the to see if it has flavor.

21. If the toilet lid is up, that means the kitty is allowed to play with the water.

22. If you are in bed and they kitty jumps up there to see you, and rewards your existence by petting your face, don't ask "Why are your paws wet?"

23. Christmas trees come from nature. It is a cat's nature to climb a tree. Thusly, do not get upset when the kitty climbs the Christmas tree.

24. Kitties enjoy sparkly, shiny things. Sparkly, shiny things hanging on a Christmas tree are a feline magnet. Do not get upset if the kitty plays with the sparkly, shiny things dangling on the Christmas tree.

25. If you place your dresser (or other tall objects upon which the kitty can jump) near a light switch, and the kitty learns to turn the lights on and off, the appropriate reaction is "Good job!" even if the kitty demonstrates this talent at 3 a.m.

26. If your kitty eats dry food, and any part of the bottom of his dry food dish is visible, do not mock the kitty when he requests that you add more food. Just do it. Visible food dish bottoms are highly distressing.

27. When a kitty jumps on your lap while you

are singing to yourself, and he places a paw across your lips, that means STOP. You are not the next American Idol.

28. Waking a person up in the morning is a Divine Feline Right, even if it involves a kitty sticking his entire nose up one pf the people's nostrils.

29. If a kitty learns to curl his paw into a fist and then punches you in the eye to wake you up, the proper reaction is "Aren't you a clever kitty!" It is not "What the -<insert your favorite bad word here>-!"

30. If a kitty wakes you up by bouncing on your bladder, don't get mad at the kitty. It's your own fault for drinking so much before bedtime. Drink less, and pet the kitty.

31. The kitty is *always* right.

And Now

For Your Viewing Pleasure

We Present

Kitties Of The Blogosphere...

(go ahead, turn the page...
...we're a pretty bunch, we are)

We Are Still The Kitties...

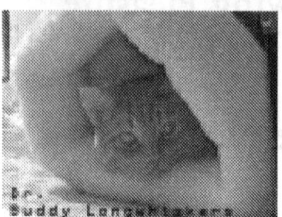
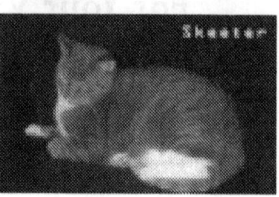
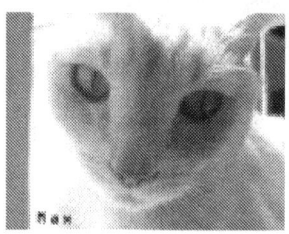

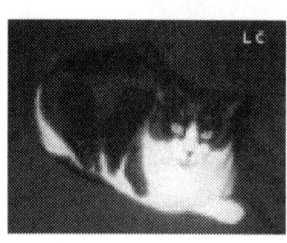

And We Writed You This Book

And We Writed You This Book 193

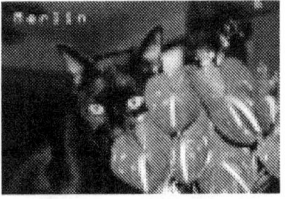

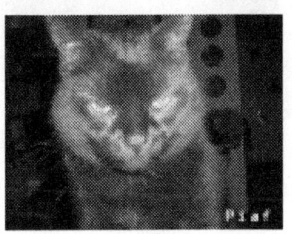

We Are Still The Kitties...

Bogey

Rex de Psychokitty

France Cat

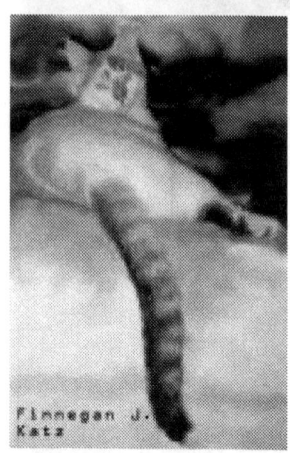
Finnegan J. Katz

Janima Dust Bunny

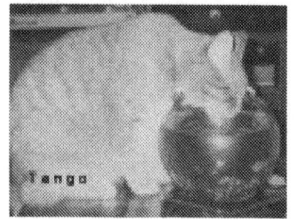
Tango

Victor Tabbycat

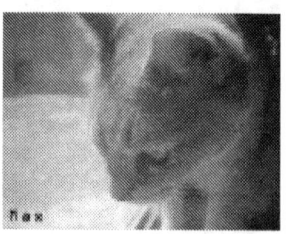
Max

And We Writed You This Book

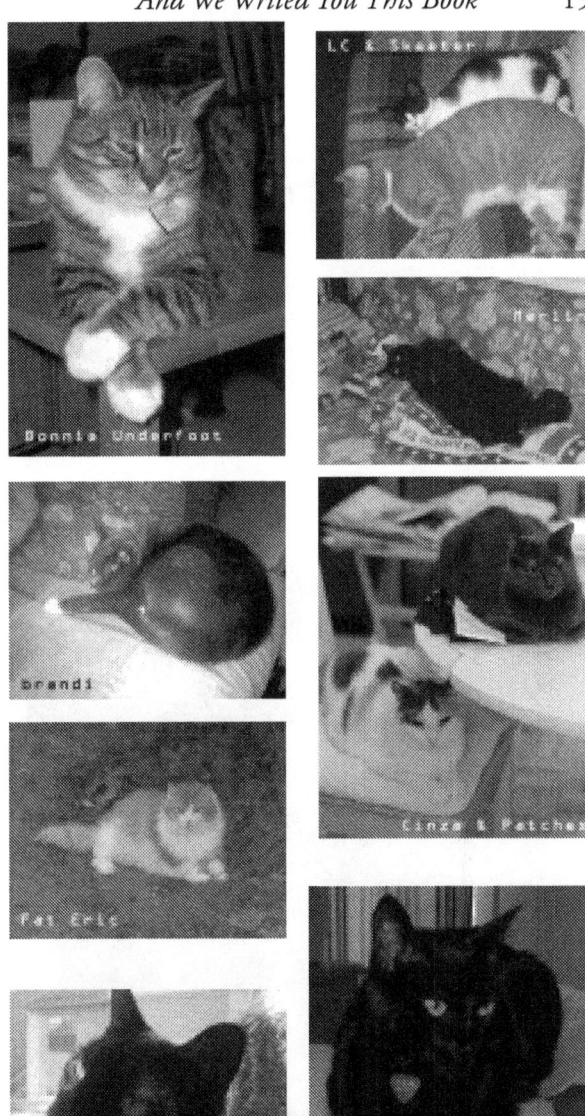

We Are Still The Kitties...

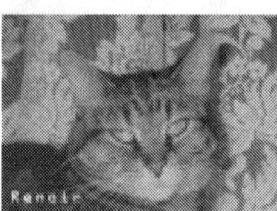

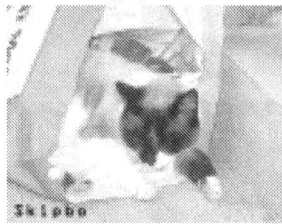

Really…
It's over

Go take a nap

Or play with the kitty

Just close the book now

You're still here

Got any crunchy treats?

The kitty would like some

There you go...that's a good People

Your kitty thanks you
We thank you
Bye Bye

www.ingramcontent.com/pod-product-compliance
Lightning Source LLC
Chambersburg PA
CBHW070639050426
42451CB00008B/221